The Emergence of The Relationship Economy

The New Order of Things to Come

with Foreword by Doc Searls, Co-Author of ***The Cluetrain Manifesto***

Scott Allen
Jay T. Deragon
Margaret G. Orem
Carter F. Smith

20660 Stevens Creek Blvd.
Suite 210
Cupertino, CA 95014

The Emergence of The Relationship Economy:
The New Order of Things to Come

First Printing: February 2008
Paperback ISBN: 1-60005-081-6 (978-1-60005-081-7)
Place of Publication: Silicon Valley, California, USA
Paperback Library of Congress Number: 2008921419

eBook ISBN: 1-60005-082-4 (978-1-60005-082-4)

Trademarks

All terms mentioned in this book that are known to be trademarks or service marks have been appropriately capitalized. Happy About® cannot attest to the accuracy of this information. Use of a term in this book should not be regarded as affecting the validity of any trademark or service mark.

Warning and Disclaimer

Every effort has been made to make this book as complete and as accurate as possible, but no warranty of fitness is implied. The information provided is on an "as is" basis. The authors and the publisher shall have neither liability nor responsibility to any person or entity with respect to an loss or damages arising from the information contained in this book.

Endorsements

"This book moves online connections into the new era of Social Networks. 'The Emergence of The Relationship Economy' is the first book to bridge face-to-face and computer-mediated relationships."

Susan B. Barnes, Professor, Associate Director, Lab for Social Computing

"I have nearly 900 'close friends' on LinkedIn. These are people I know or know now because I felt they belonged in my social network. I've had coffee or beer with a few of them but I still count most of them as close friends... close enough to be able to ask them a question without hesitation or introduce them to someone I know. They are my social network.

Social networks let people build communities of people. They are interconnected networks where you all have something in common—each other. Social networking sites create a place where you can introduce your friends to your friends' friends, where you can share your intellectual wealth. 'The Emergence of The Relationship Economy' encompasses the why and how of social networks. The authors offer a detailed look into the inner workings of social network platforms and examine how adults are adopting the tools of youth to transform the wisdom and relationships of adulthood. Business executives should use this book to understand why it is important to embrace these new tools because their employees will eventually demand them."

Joel Barrett, Solutions Architect, Cisco Systems, Inc.

"Establishing, cultivating, and maintaining relationships are key to any career or business plan. Accomplishing your goals is not impossible without good relationships, but it sure is a lot easier when you have a good personal network you can tap in order to find win-win situations for yourself that includes others in a meaningful way. 'The Emergence of The Relationship Economy' takes a comprehensive look at why this concept is of growing importance in our increasingly interconnected world. Providing thoughtful analysis on many different axes in this space, it is an interesting and useful read for just about anybody."

Pete Johnson, HP.com Chief Architect, Hewlett-Packard Company

"'The Emergence of The Relationship Economy' is the ultimate resource for those responsible for the strategic direction of their companies who wish to understand the realities and challenges presented by the upcoming Relationship Economy."

Ivan Misner, NY Times Bestselling author and Founder of BNI

"Congratulations Jay, Scott, Margaret, and Carter for producing an exceptional magnum opus!!!

I am very proud of all of you and know that counter to the chaos in the social networking sphere you have at the least made a noble attempt to make some sense of it all.

Of course there is a Relationship Economy and it's here now. What your book will do is set the framework to begin to grasp the fundamentals from the chaos and provide certain clarity where none existed before.

I highly recommend purchasing this book because of the balance and peace of mind that comes with choices. The book provides the choices and allows the reader to think for themselves."

Michael Pokocky, Futurist, Philosopher, Noted Author, and Artist

"Link To Your World and its principals have hit the evolving issues dead center. I will look forward to getting their book, 'The Emergence of The Relationship Economy,' and, knowing the depth and talent of this group, I would assume many more breakthrough insights and product offerings which we as operators can use for the benefit of our members. The social networking space clearly needs some guidance, and it is thought leaders like Link To Your World that can provide the independent viewpoints that users will respect and follow."

Thomas Power, Chairman, Ecademy

Dedication

This book is dedicated to those who are creating *The Relationship Economy*—the millions of users who have discovered the freedom of expression, the power of relationships and forged ahead in creating influences that surpass the power and reach of traditional media.

It should also be noted that the dozens of friends, associates, contributors and all those that have provided us feedback are the ones creating the fringes of change spoken of throughout this book.

Lastly and certainly not least, to our families for supporting us through this effort and understanding our passion for paving the way for The Relationship Economy to emerge.

May this book bring you new insights and the inspiration to create the world you want and the relationships you desire.

Acknowledgements

This book was created with the support of individuals in our global, virtual social networks whose postings were a source of information and inspiration.

We give special thanks to our contributing authors, Matthew Hodgson and Adam J. Kovitz, as well as Mark Kerrigan, owner of On the Mark Writing and Michael Pokocky, Futurist, Philosopher, Noted Author, and Artist for their commitment to this project. Matthew Hodgson, author of the chapter on *The Cultural Factors*, is the Regional-Lead for Web and Information Management with SMS Management & Technology Limited, Canberra, Australia. Adam J. Kovitz, author of the chapter on *The Relationship Capital Factors*, is Founder and Publisher of *The National Networker*, and is the Executive Director of the Relationship Networking Industry Association (RNIA).

In addition, we thank the founders, owners, and managers of the platforms and technology supporting our virtual connections. If it were not for the emergence of these mediums, we would not have had the opportunity to share our interest in social media.

Contents

Foreword by Doc Searls

Back in the year 2000, I found myself sitting in a plane next to a Nigerian pastor named Sayo. We were both on book junkets. I was a co-author of The Cluetrain Manifesto, which was on its way to becoming a business bestseller. Sayo had just translated The Bible to his native language of Yoruba, and sure to become an important work in his culture as well. We talked about many things, including the original meaning of markets, which had been a central topic in Cluetrain, that was becoming well-known for its first thesis: "Markets are conversations." Sayo said that was an important insight, but that it didn't go far enough.

To demonstrate, he asked me to imagine being a visitor to a public market in a less "developed" country such as his own. He picked up one of those blue airline pillows and led me on a Socratic journey. As best I can remember, our dialog went like this...

"Let's imagine this is a coat, and that you're interested in buying it. What's the first thing you say to the seller?"

"What does it cost?"

"Yes, you would say that, because where you come from, it's natural to see everything in a market moving toward a transaction. Now let's say the vendor tells you the price is fifty dollars. What happens next?"

"We bargain until we arrive at a price between what he asks and what I'm willing to pay."

"Yes. Again, that's typical of what somebody from your culture would say. But today you're also saying 'Markets are conversations.' So let's say you get into a conversation with the seller that's not about the price. Let's say you know a lot about textiles, about manufacturing and distribution, about dyes and fashion. And let's say the vendor tells you about the craftsman who made the garment, the material used, the origins of that material, the culture expressed in the design and the weave, the means by which the garment arrived at the market. And let's say you both gain a lot from each other's knowledge in the course of the conversation."

"Okay."

"What happens to the price?"

"I may end up wanting to pay more while he wants to charge less."

"Yes. And why is that?"

"I'm not sure."

"It's because you now have a *relationship*. When you look at a public market in my culture from the perspective of yours, you tend to see it through the prism of transaction, surrounded by the noise of conversation, within which the only talk that matters is negotiation toward a final price. But if all you see and hear is bargaining, you miss most of what's really going on."

He went on to explain that three things happen in all "natural" markets: transaction, conversation and relationship. In our "developed" culture, we understand transaction almost to an excessive degree, because to us, as we so often say, "It all comes down to the bottom line." But, Sayo added, our understanding of markets is inadequate around conversation and utterly impoverished around relationship.

He said he was sure we actually do have, and value, relationships; but because we understand and value them so little we'd tend to abandon relationships when times get tough, and to rationalize our decisions in terms of transactional value alone.

That's why the next frontier for "developed" economies, he said, was relationship. We need to explore and unpack that topic, or we'll stay stuck in an inadequate understanding of what markets really are—and how much they embody life in all is true richness and variety.

At the end of our conversation, he gave me an assignment. He told me that the next book I write should be about how "Markets are relationships" at least as much as they are conversations and transactions.

I never got around to writing that book, although I've focused intensively on market relationships ever since meeting Sayo. That focus is what led me to meeting and getting to know Scott Allen, Jay Deragon and Carter Smith. And now it pleases me to say that these three men together with Margaret Orem have written the book Sayo assigned me to write. They have explored and unpacked what's most important and least understood about markets, and have outlined in fine detail the economy that will grow out of relationships in what Cluetrain called the "networked" marketplace.

Like the markets Sayo calls "natural," the networked marketplace turns out to be a profoundly social one that can only be enlarged and improved by relationships. The Web, it turns out, is what the authors call The Human Network.

We're all in it. And not just for ourselves. That's what makes it so valuable.

Doc Searls
Berkman Fellow and co-author of the business best-seller **'The Cluetrain Manifesto: The End of Business as Usual'**

Preface

The convergence of technology that accelerates the power of relationships and facilitates dynamic communications—peer to peer and to entire communities—is revolutionary to say the least.

The book defines The Relationship Economy as "The people and things we are connected with in our personal networks, who or that distribute or consume our capital, which in turn influences our individual production outputs." The book analyzes the factors that are influencing an emerging economy based on the sum of factors driving massive and significant changes to the way everyone will work, play, and live.

This emergence will have an especially profound effect on businesses and individuals. While individual factors are self-evident, the collective factors, taken as a whole, are the basis for individual conclusions for strategic opportunities that can be gained from the new economy.

The book provides the knowledge, tools, and suggested skills necessary for improved comprehension of the strategic issues required to succeed in The Relationship Economy, and provides the context of actions that enable success. It covers an emerging opportunity for the global community of users/consumers/citizens, consumer brands, corporations, non-governmental organizations, and governments to play a critical role in forging this new carbon-neutral economy: The Relationship Economy.

This book details an emerging economy, driven by factors that are affecting massive changes to the way people work, play, and live. This emergence will have an especially profound effect on business. While individual factors are self-evident, when taken collectively, they are the basis that individuals use to identify strategic opportunities to be gained from the new economy.

This book is a foundational resource for individuals and entities to use as each begins to plan for participation in the accelerated changes brought on my technological advances of the World Wide Web. The goal of the book is to enable all parties to gain perspective, knowledge, and insight as to the dynamics of technology, the impact of changes brought on by the social Web, and what factors should be considered for the purposes of planning for success.

Introduction

The Web is steadily becoming a utility of the masses. We have become familiar with using the Web for communicating, surfing, shopping, receiving information in different forms, and a host of other usage attributes—both personal and professional.

The Web economy has largely been fed by advertisers vying for eyeballs and attention. Advertisers have been a fundamental resource of the Web economy. When a change occurs that alters the old models and creates improved models with a promise of higher returns, then changes are likely to create systemic shifts across the entire Web that influence the system from end to end.

Innovation inevitably spawns further innovation throughout the supply chain of interconnected elements that fuel Web usage patterns, and the social Web facilitates systemic changes, which are fueled through such innovation. The social Web brings more influential human elements with global reach than any previous technological development in the history of the Web. Combine the influence of the human elements with the economic power of relationship driven commerce and you have a scenario that will create further changes unforeseen, unpredictable, and unimaginable.

These changes are profound and create historical shifts that open opportunities for those who prepare and embrace the factors that enable a successful transition from the old economy to the new.

This book is organized around a discussion of Key Factors, each covered in its own chapter, which describes the influences, benefits, and related outcomes created by the emergence of The Relationship Economy.

Each chapter addresses the value-add each factor brings to the emergence of The Relationship Economy, including how parties will be able to leverage those benefits for economic gains through transformation of relationship mediums and positions. This book identifies components that are constant in this market and how these constants can be used as the fundamental basis for a continuously changing planning process. The chapters can be used as stand-alone references or in consideration with the totality of the book.

The collective content findings include:

- The convergence of social media and technological advances is creating a new medium for economic exchanges.

- Individuals, corporations, institutions, organizations, and governments will all play a vital role in the emerging relationship economy.

- The Relationship Economy will disrupt many traditional mediums and media.

- The Relationship Economy will emerge quickly, and billions of dollars of economic exchange will continually shift between multiple markets and millions of individuals.

- The Relationship Economy leverages the efficiency and effectiveness of the ability to reach one-to-one and one-to-millions, both online and through mobile connectivity.

- The Relationship Economy appeals to the basic human needs and fulfills many of the current societal caps. It reverses many of the current strains on the quality and qualitative issues facing humanity today.

- Numerous factors that surround the emergence of a Relationship Economy are converging, and in some instances, colliding. The content provides insights into the initial and critical converging factors.

Corporations will find significant insights that will enable them to strategically plan for the substantial shifts caused by the emergence of The Relationship Economy.

Technology Vendors will garner intelligence that will assist them in the development and deployment of social media and social networking applications, infrastructure, analytics, and advertising platforms.

Media Companies will benefit from informed perspectives regarding changes they will need to make in order to increase the reach and richness of their brands.

Network Devices Vendors will learn how to use the concept of The Relationship Economy to facilitate increased sales of routers, servers, and other critically important devices.

Wireless Carriers will find methods for coping with the changes to their traditional businesses and will understand how to "turn the retreat into a parade."

Educators will learn how the instructional yield from one-to-one computing will be multiplied and significantly altered by the dynamics of The Relationship Economy and will be able to share that knowledge.

Government and Private Institutions will be able to capitalize on the new abilities that will be ushered in by The Relationship Economy, which will enable them to reach and effectively communicate with constituents and legislators

Individuals will become aware of the benefits of embracing the changes that are fueling The Relationship Economy and how to leverage opportunities to expand relationship capital for economic gains. They will be empowered with new knowledge.

Learning and preparing for historical change can sometimes be overwhelming. The authors of this book have aimed at providing its readers with a comprehensive understanding of the dynamics of the shifts currently happening—and those to come. These shifts promise to be extremely disruptive for age-old business institutions and models, and the underlying economic factors that will affect all of us globally.

The authors' objectives are to provide support to those who want to be prepared and to capture explosive opportunities. As such, the authors will be happy to answer any questions and provide further directions for our readers.

You may reach out to the authors and contact them individually by looking up their profiles on LinkedIn and Facebook, or contact them through Link to Your World at
http://www.linktoyourworld.com.

May you be blessed with abundance in the new economy—The Relationship Economy!

1 A Revolution has Begun

Jay T. Deragon

Social computing and the medium of social networks are creating a revolution that is similar to the industrial revolution of the 19th century in its impact on commerce, but on a global scope. This communication revolution includes the development of advanced communications tools and proxies, such as Skype.

Today politics, products, and services are virtually consumer/user-led developments. Google is a major example of a user-generated brand where the users have suggested and embraced enhancements. Current technology is so pervasive that it has become quite significant in the political realm. With cutting-edge communication systems, national political groups and institutions in the United States of America are lobbying with influential bloggers to inform and educate the voter, as well as impact public opinion.

There is an opportunity for the global community of users, consumers, citizens, consumer brands, corporations, non-governmental organizations, and governments to play a critical role in forging this new carbon-neutral economy, The Relationship Economy (Searls, 2007).

To begin to comprehend what the new economy will look like, watch the young people in your organization—particularly the ones who are fresh out of college. They have lived their entire lives in the digital age, communicating in real-time via text messaging and instant messages. For some of them, even email lacks the immediate gratification they expect when they want to communicate with someone. To this generation, the desktop phone has about as much relevance as an electric typewriter does for those of us a generation or two older.

Using cutting-edge communications technologies, this younger generation has created online communities based on shared interests. They keep in constant contact with the people they care about, no matter where they are located. They create, collect, and share digital content and information—music, pictures, news, video. It is all a testament to the power and immediacy of today's digital technology.

It is also a perfect breeding ground for continued development of The Relationship Economy (Searls, 2007). Instead of online communities based on shared interests, when these digital-age individuals join your company, they will build virtual work teams that span the globe. The list of important people they keep in touch with will expand to include your customers. In addition to music and pictures, they will share reports and presentations created in collaboration with colleagues and business partners.

As this generation moves into the workforce, they expect to continue using the devices they have grown up with and depended upon for communication and production. Organizations that cannot meet this expectation will be at a sharp disadvantage as talented young people choose to work for companies that recognize the value of a new generation of communications innovations.

Companies that do embrace the new economy framework will see incredible benefits. Recruiting young talent will be easier, of course. However, the gains will be much broader. Advanced social computing technology will help companies raise productivity and respond more rapidly to changing business conditions. These technologies will also enable organizations to create closer ties to customers, develop innovative products more quickly, and reduce costs.

Ultimately, The Relationship Economy is a new business model that recognizes that people—not processes—are the most significant component. Moreover, it is about allowing technology to unleash the passion and potential that each one of us brings with us every day when we go to work.

To understand the concept of The Relationship Economy, it is important to start with a basic understanding of the terminology. The word "relationship" is defined as a connection or an association; the condition of being related. The word "economy" is defined as the study of resource allocation, distribution, and consumption; of capital and investment; and of management of the factors of individual production. For purposes of discussion in this book, we will define the term "capital" as that which we give or take that creates numerous forms of value.

Therefore, we define The Relationship Economy as:
The people and things we are connected with in our personal networks, who or that distribute or consume our capital, which in turn influences our individual production outputs.

The Relationship Economy will transform existing business models. Corporations will experience a major change to a virtual workforce, and the emergence of new leaders will come from smaller firms. In this forthcoming era, the big will become small and the small will become big. New rules for The Relationship Economy will create significant global shifts in economics, governments, and institutions—in effect, creating a society with no borders and no boundaries (Kelly, 1998).

Peter F. Drucker, author of over 35 books, Presidential Medal of Freedom winner, and a leading voice in the business world, sums up the drastic changes on the horizon in the business world:

"The corporation as we know it, which is now 120 years old, is unlikely to survive the next 25 years. Legally and financially yes, but not structurally and economically." Peter Drucker, quoted in Business 2.0, August 22, 2000 (The Rhythm of Business, 2006)

Evidence abounds that Professor Drucker's prediction is a reality; the world of business is changing fundamentally. What is next? The rise of The Relationship Economy fueled by advanced social computing technologies.

Emerging Shifts in Focus

Business-Centric Companies	Relationship-Focused Economy
Product-centric	Relationship-centric
Win-lose	Win-win
Control	Transparency
Periodic	Real time
Brand	Reputation
Excessive-promise	Trust
Mass communications	Conversations
Pyramid/silo	Network of relationships
Transactions	Relationships
Only money matters	All sources of value count

Jay Deragon : www.linktoyourworld.com

This new economy is part of a relationship-centric matrix that draws on the very foundations of human behavior and American psychologist Abraham Maslow's Hierarchy of Needs (Sørensen, 2006). The growth of adult adoption of social computing technologies creates a new dynamic unlike that of MySpace. These new networks address specific elements of adult relationships and concentrate primarily on business needs, wherein sites such as MySpace have focused on the social networking needs of young adults.

What Motivates Adult Participation in On-line Social Networks?

When we look at the psychology of human behavior, we can begin to understand certain baseline motivations that draw adults to online social networks. Abraham Maslow published his theory of human motivation in 1943. Its popularity continues unabated. Like his colleague Carl Rogers, Maslow, who also wrote the 1954 book *Motivation and Personality*, believed that actualization was the driving force of human personality. Maslow's great insight was to place actualization into a hierarchy of motivation.

Self-actualization, as he called it, is the highest drive, but before a person can turn to it, he or she must satisfy other, lower motivations such as hunger, safety, and belonging. The hierarchy has five levels.

1. **Physiological:** hunger, thirst, shelter, sex, etc.

2. **Safety:** security, protection from physical and emotional harm

3. **Social:** affection, belonging, acceptance, friendship

4. **Esteem (also called ego):** self respect, autonomy, achievement (internal); and status, recognition, and attention (external)

5. **Self-actualization:** doing things

Maslow points out that the hierarchy is dynamic; the dominant need is always shifting. The hierarchy does not exist by itself, but it is affected by the situation and the general culture. Satisfaction is relative. Douglas McGregor (1960) makes the hierarchy the building block for his Theory X and Theory Y. Mihalyi Csikszentmihalyi (1993) also uses the hierarchy in his concept of "flow." A 1990s example of self-actualization may be surfing the Internet.

Empirical research has confirmed the first three levels, but has not done so for the fourth and fifth levels of esteem and self-actualization. Some have noted that Maslow's hierarchy follows the life cycle. A newborn baby's needs are largely physiological. As the baby grows, it needs safety, then love. Toddlers are eager for social interaction. Teenagers are anxious about social needs; young adults are concerned with esteem, and only more mature people transcend the first four levels to spend much time self-actualizing.

Based on the observations across numerous networking platforms and reflection on the past definitions of human motivation, it is clear that online social networks provide a primary motivation for adults in the category of self-actualization, or *doing things*. Maslow defines self-actualization as growth-motivated rather than deficiency-motivated (Sørensen, 2006).

What Things Are Adults Doing Within Social Networks That Enhance Individual Growth?

Based on observations and interviews, we will provide a general categorization of the factors that enhance individual growth for adults participating in online social networks. These factors will be defined in greater detail in future articles.

The Learning Factors: With all the hype, craze, and media coverage of social networking platforms such as Facebook and LinkedIn, many adults are drawn to the medium to learn what is causing the hype.

The Connection Factors: Once adults enter networks and learn the "tools of the trade," many are amazed to find the presence of other adults they know and the volume of people that they do not know who already engage with social media or the enabling mediums.

The Affinity Factors: Adults begin to find association with groups, causes, forums, media, and other affinities that relate to their interests, both personally and professionally.

The Business Factors: One of the predominant business segments using social networks today is employment recruiters. As the medium and the adult participation in social media increase, business opportunities grow exponentially. Adults are rapidly learning to use social networks as their medium.

The Creative Factors: Adults, and their businesses, are applying creative ways to use the technology behind social computing to extend its value to both personal and professional needs.

The Expectation Factors: When you consider the creative possibilities of social networks, adults expect some economic and social value to be derived from their participation, whether currently or in the future.

The expectation of individual growth and satisfaction is high. These factors, combined with the media hype over social networking, are the motivating issues that are driving millions of adults to the medium at annual growth rates of 70% and more. The opportunity to capitalize economically is emerging quickly. Word of mouth will fuel growth rates faster than any other technological medium in our past. The growth and related factors will usher in The Relationship Economy.

References

Csikszentmihalyi, M. (1993). *Flow: The Psychology of Optimal Experience.* New York: Harper & Row.

Kelly, K. (1998). *New Rules for the New Economy.* Retrieved September 1, 2007, from http://www.kk.org/newrules

McGregor, D. (1960). *The Human Side of Enterprise.* New York: McGraw-Hill.

Searls, D. (2007). Building an Relationship Economy. http://www.linuxjournal.com/node/1000182 referencing *The Cluetrain Manifesto,* Retrieved October 17, 2007, from http://cluetrain.com

Sørensen, K. (2006). *Maslow's hierarchy of needs and subpersonality work.* Retrieved October 17, 2007, from http://two.not2.org/psychosynthesis/articles/maslow.htm

The Rhythm of Business (2006). *Leading Thoughts for the New Era of Relationship Business*. Retrieved November 20, 2007, from http://www.rhythmofbusiness.com/LeadingThoughts/Default.asp

2 The Time Factors

Jay T. Deragon

With so many demands vying for our time and attention, sometimes even a simple, uninterrupted phone call seems to be a stretch of the imagination. Cell phones, personal digital assistants (PDAs), instant messaging, pagers, faxes, emails—and the list goes on—all contribute to information availability and overload. To participate in The Relationship Economy will also require this valuable commodity: our time.

The very essence of the emerging Relationship Economy is in the name: Relationship. Relationships take time. In Western society, we have been trained to "want what we want, when we want it—five minutes ago." Our society of "instants"—from microwavable foods to lightning-speed Internet searches to 24/7 news channels—have conditioned us to move and produce at an extremely fast pace.

With so much information surrounding us, along with our trained passion for quick answers, we often miss the value of learning and creating relationships. Those of us who learn to optimize our attention have a significant advantage in this high-input, high-speed world. Engaging the attention of others is pivotal; it leads to personal leverage, which, in turn, leads to the power to influence behavior.

Social Networking enables massive personal leverage. Through social networking, an individual can reach the masses, and give to them rather than reaching just a few. Those who accomplish the greatest amount of personal influence will be those who gain the most in The Relationship Economy. Those who transform their thinking, and trust in the essence of human relations, will create social and business value faster than ever before. The dynamics we are all facing become the Paradox of Choice, i.e., a question of where we should give our most valuable asset: time.

The Effects of Increased Access to Information

As more information and choices become available and accessible, individuals will need to hone their skills in coping and in making good decisions and choices. Additional information and choice are inevitable, as each new day adds to humanities' data bank and cannot be halted. It is important to examine the demands on time in order to understand how important "The Time Factors" are in productivity and self-fulfillment.

A Reuters' survey of 1,300 business people revealed that two-thirds of the respondents' personal relationships have been affected by the amount of information available. These respondents also experience more tension at work and feel less satisfied with their jobs due to the quantity of information. Forty percent feel that an abundance of information can delay important decisions and hampers the ability to make good decisions. Nonetheless, two out of three respondents said they wanted even more information! (Waddington, 1996)

The "too much information" complaint is not unique to any one social networking site. Actually, it has spurred similar issues across most social networking sites. Andrew LaVallee (2007) writes in the Wall Street Journal:

> Brooklyn Web designer Pete Jelliffe, 26, has deactivated links to friends whose check-ins filled his cell phone with text messages, and has been similarly delisted, he suspects, by an ex-girlfriend.

"I've blocked people that, say, signed up and just added me because we were acquaintances," he said. "I guess they liked me more than I liked them, and I didn't care to hear about them that frequently." (p. 2)

As more and more adults move onto Facebook, similar issues are beginning to appear. A never-ending proliferation of groups is forming, and members are inviting all their friends, most of whom are on other networks, to join. New applications launch daily, which only spawns more invitations from contacts wishing to share their newfound tool with their contacts. Social networking sites are getting feature- and function-rich, while on many sites, users are being "dinged" with overage charges or denied the ability to add the connections they wish to add.

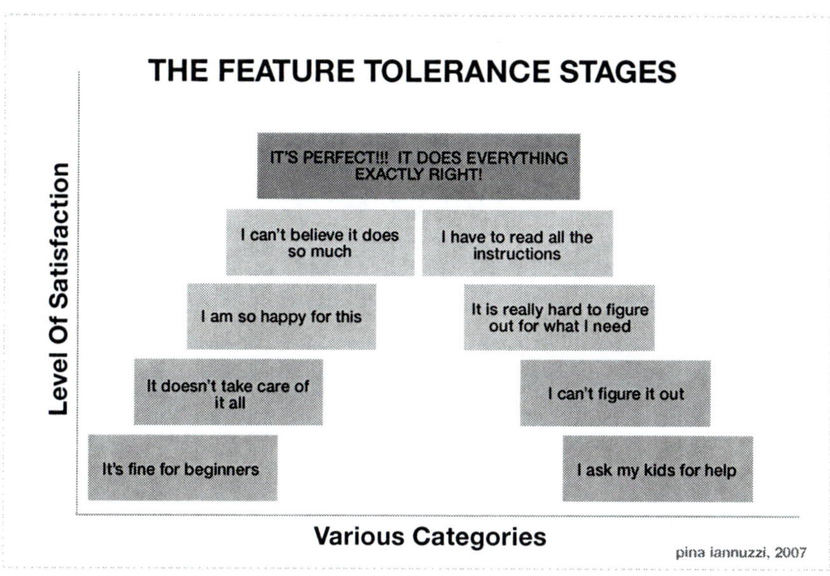

While all this technology may seem "cool" at first, it quickly wears on the minds and pocketbooks of users, including opportunity cost and the costs associated with paying for memberships, features, etc. The frustration levels increase as the number of choices increase. Worst of all, it is difficult to learn how to leverage all these features into personal and professional (economic) gain, such as new business, product sales, etc. The growth of social networks is staggering and it appears to be in a period of unlimited choices for individuals.

Social networking technologies develop a momentum of their own, which takes individuals way beyond the point of *counterproductivity* to the point of *self-defeat*. While the phenomena of social networking technologies appeals to some of our basic human needs it also appeals to human weaknesses, such as the need for instant-gratification, and reveals our insatiable appetites.

What are the individual's objectives? Much of the convenience of social networking occurs by inconveniencing others. The craze for having a large network, for example, appeals to the competitive nature of human beings to be the biggest, most connected individual in any one network. People spend countless hours building the numbers in their network, ignoring the quality of those relationships.

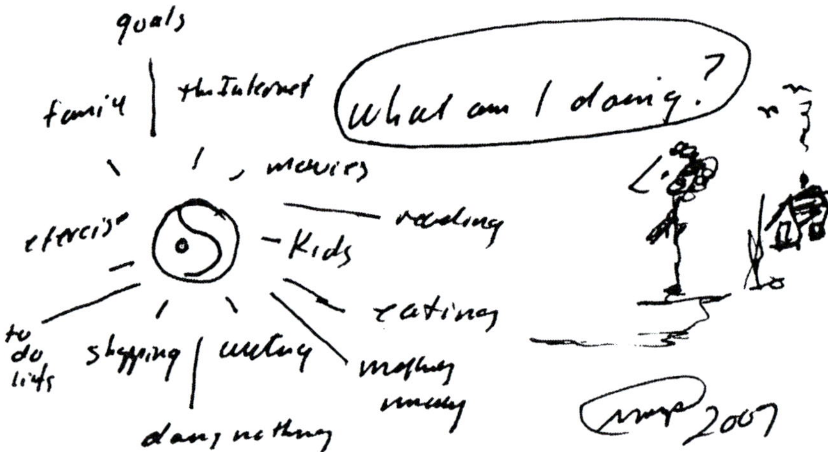

Michael Pokocky, Copyright © 2007

The Hidden Game Appeal. The phenomenon of social networking is intriguing for many adults, and they spend countless hours engaged in the game. Owners, developers, and operators of social networking sites understand the appeal of new technology when it is designed around the human desire to be aware—if not on the cutting edge—of

     Chapter 2: The Time Factors

new ideas and technology. Knowing this, owners launch new, targeted networks with the latest gizmos and gadgets that will increase their attraction to the masses.

The people, both young and old, follow the appeal, and the cycle of intrigue is designed to keep the masses engaged. Network operators are motivated to establish technological relationships with their customer with the aim of drawing in the masses so the network's economic value increases.

Case in point. One moderator of several dozen forums spent several years moderating hundreds of discussions and encouraging individuals to use and make the best use of a particular social network. There was no economic return compensation for his loyalty or efforts. Was the network obligated to pay a moderator who invested such time and energy for his efforts? No, but if that social network was interested in improving its relationship with the many thousands of users of those forums, it would have been reasonable for them to have recognized the value and provided some economic support. The lesson here is to maintain and cultivate relationships and to maximize the opportunity to create good will. In the end, it saves time because you will not have to search for and create new connections.

Enslavement or Enablement? What makes technological advancements unique is that they are intended to enhance peoples' lives (save time). However, some people become enslaved by the technology while others figure out ways to be enabled. Those who create the technology do so with a purpose. The purpose is to make money, using technology to appeal to the human and business needs that drive mass adoption. Much of the marketing buzz about technology promotes its benefit, but never do we see the scope of our cost for adopting the latest and greatest technological advances. Using technology can become detrimental to our time, our relations, and our economic standing if we do not invest mindfully with a view to a financially viable outcome. Further, using technology can provide opportunities to leverage the medium for our own individual gains. Our gains must be definable and useful to our individual purposes.

About one half of all working adults (52%) use Social Networking within their companies for their work with colleagues in their company, while 47% also use it in their work with clients (Vickers, 2007). Further, Social

Networking increases the expertise of a company. More than half of those questioned (55%) said that they use it in order to share the experiences of high performers in their teams with others, and 49% use it in order to solve current problems *as soon as possible.*

Social Network technology and dynamics are being modeled by some as a viable business cost that will improve productivity, and thereby save time within corporations.

However, some companies are preventing access to Facebook from their intranets because of fear of losing productivity and concerns over security. Companies should be aware of and concerned about particular risk factors, but appropriate management of Internet use significantly reduces potential problems.

We may waste time searching for the perfect network solution from both a personal and business standpoint. Social networks vary in size, composition, approach, features, membership requirements, personal profile layouts, etc. There are many opinions on the right way to do it. What ends up happening is we go out looking for the "right" way to do things, and often finding ourselves going down a rabbit trail of confusion that ultimately leads to inaction.

The stronger our belief that there is a perfect solution out there (whatever we have deemed to be "perfect"), the more we end up searching for it—wasting more time than necessary or appropriate. As a result, we are less likely to be satisfied with our final decision because it will rarely live up to our unrealistic expectations.

Another consistent time waster is the belief that more is always better than less. We join more networks, learning about and using more technology with the mistaken belief that all of this activity will pay off in the end. Unfortunately, the truth is the polar opposite. As the number of networking tactics climbs, mastery in any of them plummets, and online and this can prove costly. As the social networking space explodes, we are swamped with invitations to join numerous networks, and most of the time it is from people with whom we are already connected in another network.

We have all become information/content producers, skilled in generating information. No one has the time to manage all the information produced and to determine which information is useful and not wasteful, or, even worse, destructive. The net result is that when we try to get our work done, information may seem to get in our way. We tend to spend more time getting lost in the sea of information and its relevance than we spend in the actual collection of pertinent information. Until convergence happens and we usher in a true Relationship Economy, the increasing volume of information will diminish and stymie our productivity.

During the information age, having more information meant having more power. For a while, it held true—until the amount of information exploded and the Internet leveled the playing field regarding the access to information.

The psychologist David Lewis, who analyzed the findings of Paul Waddington's 1996 Reuter Business' survey, proposed the term *Information Fatigue Syndrome* to describe the resulting symptoms, which include, among others, an inability to make analytical decisions without increased doubt or anxiety and the willingness to blame others instead of taking responsibility (Lewis, 1999).

Other side effects highlighted by Lewis (1999) include anxiety, poor decision-making, difficulties in remembering, and reduced attention span. The more information we try to suck in, the more we train ourselves to default to a shorter attention span. Thus, the more information we have and get, the less time we have to get things done.

However, not all is lost in this increasing maze of information and choice. As we begin to recognize that there will continue to be an accumulation of information and choice, we will seek methods, systems, and advice as to how to successfully select, manage, and use the information and choices that make social media the great vehicle it is. With learning and experience, such individuals will have an increased capacity to cope and manage.

References

LaVallee, A. (2007). Friends Swap Twitters, and Frustration: New Real-Time Messaging Services Overwhelm Some Users With Mundane Updates From Friends. *The Wall Street Journal Online*, March 16, 2007. Retrieved September 2, 2007 from http://online.wsj.com/public/article/SB117373145818634482-ZwdoP Q0PqPrcFMDHDZLz_P6osnl_20080315.html http://tinyurl.com/3bcocq

Lewis, D. (1999). *Information Overload: Practical Strategies for Surviving in Today's Workplace*. London: Penguin Books.

Pokocky, Michael (2007). Sketches used by permission. All rights reserved and provided with gracious permission to use by the authors of this book.

Vickers, M. (2007, May 29). Think Online Social Networking Is Kid Stuff? Think Again, Institute for Corporate Productivity. Retrieved January 31, 2008, from http://www.i4cp.com/i4cp/news.aspx?PostId=20200

Waddington, P. (1996). *Dying for Information? An Investigation into the Effects of Information Overload in the UK and Worldwide*. London: Reuters Business.

3 The Knowledge Factors

Carter F. Smith

Aristotle observed that all men by their nature desire knowledge. James Madison claimed that people who want self-governance must arm themselves with the power that knowledge gives. Sir Francis Bacon gave us perhaps the clearest foundation on which to build in the context of The Relationship Economy: Knowledge is power.

This inherently means that we must be careful with what we do with knowledge. Should we hold it close to ensure no one else can take it? Would it be appropriate to let others examine it as long as they do not get too close or try to alter it? The Relationship Economy model appears to demand that we share knowledge, and share it a lot. Knowledge hoarded is of no value to anyone, but knowledge transferred is priceless.

The speed of knowledge transfer is increasing. In the Internet-enabled world, knowledge develops faster, changes more quickly, and is central to the success of a variety of organizations than ever before. Every organization in the world—academic, corporate, and government—needs to adapt to those changes, and do so quickly. A tremendous paradigm shift in knowledge access and distribution is underway. While information is an essential constituent of *knowledge*, it is not knowledge in and of itself. Raw information leads to the development of theory, and when theory is applied through experience, the result is knowledge. Experience alone is insufficient without theory. The incorporation of social networking into the knowledge distribution model promises to bring some new and interesting challenges for organizations as they develop strategies to accomplish their goals and objectives. Unfortunately, many of today's leadership theories promote the silo thinking or a "one-size-fits-all" mentality. These theories will fail in their attempts to increase the knowledge base.

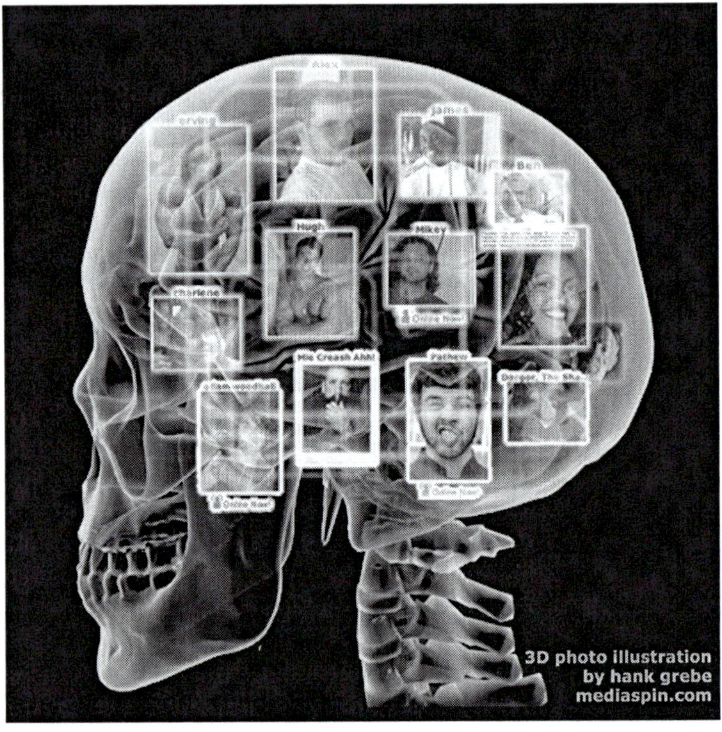

Hank Grebe, 2007

The term 'The Relationship Economy' resulted from a broader recognition of the role that knowledge and technology have in catalyzing economic growth. Knowledge has always been central to economic development when impacted by the introduction of new technology (Cimol, 2005). Those developments do not just appear out of thin air; they begin with the recognition of a perceived need, and result in providing the foundation for change. The real transforming power of the Internet exists in the breakdown it has caused in the traditional information hierarchy (Peizer, 2000).

Have we now transitioned into a new knowledge economy? If so, is the transition we are making as significant and far reaching as was the shift from an agricultural economy into the industrial revolution of barely a century ago?

In the ongoing debate on the knowledge economy, an emphasis has been placed on the role of innovation with a reliance on intellectual capabilities (Carlaw, Oxley, Walker, Thorns, and Nuth, 2006). Modern technologies are very useful for their ability to span long distances and quickly transfer large volumes of data. The development of self-organizing networked social systems generating shared knowledge is causing the standards for knowledge transfer to change even before we identify the previous standards (Wittig, nd). The rapid changes in the knowledge base are only possible with intentional collaboration, however.

Knowledge transfer is a collective and constructive activity that occurs only through network interaction. Based on an autopoietic (self-creating) model, the generation of knowledge increases through communication transfers between structurally coupled individuals and organizations (Wittig, nd). Without this transfer of information, the strength of our networks is limited to the simplicity of their connections—not the knowledge exchanged between them. As a result, our most powerful collaborations are potentially crippled by weakened connections.

So, if knowledge is power and the transfer of knowledge has value, how does knowledge actually affect The Relationship Economy?

According to Peizer (2000), unequal status of the holder and the user acts as a barrier to knowledge access. Historically, knowledge has been distributed from doctor to patient, from lawyer to client, and from teacher to student. The provider of information is often the powerbroker or gatekeeper, setting not only the criteria for access, but also the price.

The Internet has served to circumvent (or reinvent) these imbalanced, power-based relationships by removing the restrictions and leveling the playing field for those who seek information. Information is fast becoming a commodity whose value is determined by all who have access to it, changing the role of the information provider to a "value-added knowledge facilitator" (Peizer, 2000). This new classification can be incorporated into any model, and it often catalyzes the knowledge access of those who previously found it inaccessible.

So what happens when there is a level playing field? Does it create an unfilled void, or do opportunities that did not previously exist begin to open up for individuals and organizations that have the vision, comprehension, and flexibility necessary to usher in The Relationship Economy?

The rapid growth of social networks has brought a new and exciting era to the Web. Information and communication technologies are facilitating organized human endeavor in fundamentally new ways. The broad impact that social computing brings to these diverse domains, combined with the complexity of cross-discipline features, poses new challenges for those who hope to harness, or at least understand it. Research in this area should expand to include examination of multi-disciplinary theories and methodologies. Continued research on the use of social computing will produce transformative research and education (Parameswaran and Whinston, 2007).

Creating a Knowledge-Sharing Culture

Creating a "knowledge-sharing culture" is about making knowledge sharing the norm for human relationships (Gurteen, 1999). Most people naturally collaborate. When people work in a collaborative environment, it produces a knowledge-sharing culture that can be difficult for organizations to manage and understand. Only the organizations that harness the power of cooperation can effectively use knowledge to be more productive.

Remember, we are talking about strategically sharing organizational knowledge, not simply providing information as a business strategy. The ultimate purpose of strategic knowledge sharing is to allow an organization to meet its business objectives (Gurteen, 1999). Applying knowledge attained within an organization is an integral part the organization's success. Michael Schrage said, "Knowledge management is a bull issue" as "most people in most organizations do not have the ability to act on the knowledge they possess" (Gurteen, 1999). What stifles this action? It could be a lack of understanding, but more likely, it is the culture of the organization. So why not change the culture?

Change in any sense is often difficult. To change a culture is especially daunting, because it means seeing the world in a different way (Wasko and Faraj, 2000). It means intentionally revealing more of our hidden paradigms—like the tacit acceptance that "knowledge is power" (Hendler, 2005). It means the radical restructuring of thought.

So how do we start changing the culture of sharing knowledge?

Change has already begun in The Relationship Economy. The introduction of blogs counters the effects of an unsupervised media. The arrival of wikis challenges traditional communication processes because it introduces online and visible collaboration. Social networks provide a fresh look at the previously untapped power of relationships that naturally form when online communication and social communities intersect.

An influx of social computing applications and the explosion of online communities are changing the way we share information and increasing the speed with which we communicate. These technologies elicit an initial feeling of intimidation that transforms swiftly to awe. The applications are quickly changing the global economy, changing the way we interact, and affecting every aspect of our lives (Rollyson, 2006). According to a Forrester Research report, individuals in the new economy increasingly take their cues from one another and their social communities, rather than from institutional sources such as corporations (Charron, Favier and Li, 2006). As a result, communities are increasingly trying to find ways to drive innovation from the bottom up, and the ownership of experience, economic value, and authority is shifting from traditional institutions to communities of individuals (Wang, Zeng, Carley, and Mao, 2007).

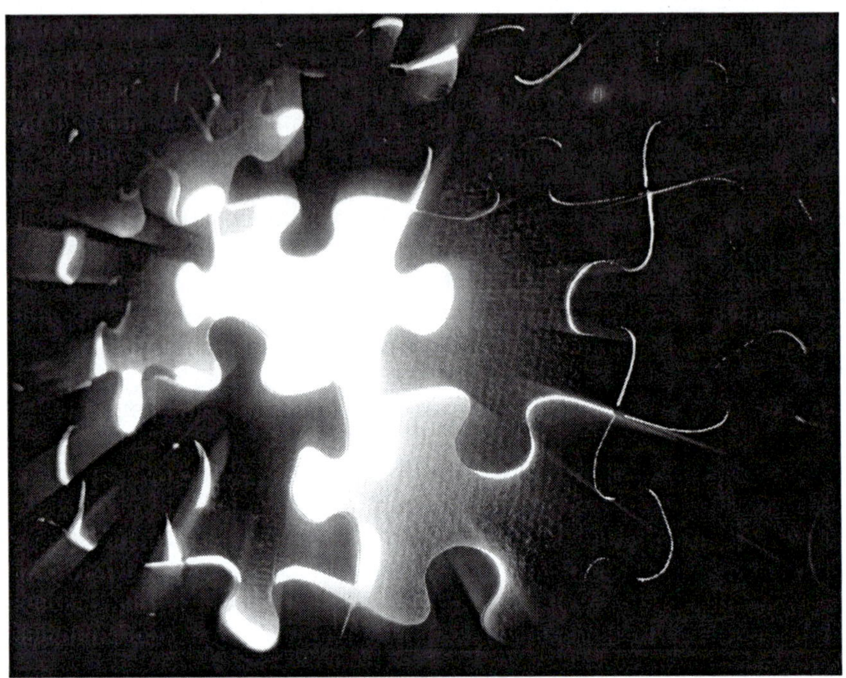

According to Valdis Krebs, an authority on social network analysis, "The effective utilization of knowledge and learning requires *both* culture and technology" (Krebs, 1998). Yet, simple data transfer, such as that found in traditional business information processes, does *not* frequently offer the competitive advantage that is so necessary for success. An organization's real edge is often found in the context-sensitive knowledge that is difficult, if not often impossible, to maintain with a simple digital storage and analysis strategy (Krebs, 1999). This core institutional knowledge lies in the minds of individuals, specialized communities, and in their connections. As Krebs (1998) stated, "An organization's *data* is found in its computer systems, but a company's *intelligence* is found in its biological and social systems." Highly developed computer networks must exist to support the social and professional networks of people in today's fluid and adaptive organizations—not social and professional networks in place to support computer networks. Krebs (1999) asked, "If knowledge is power, what is connected knowledge?" The Relationship Economy operates on the strengths and complexities of a variety of connections. The economic

                                    Chapter 3: The Knowledge Factors

considerations of networks have no place for independent (i.e., uncon-nected) objects whether they are individuals, teams, or computers (Krebs, 1999).

All individuals, communities, systems, and business assets are intercon-nected in the evolving economic Web. In The Relationship Economy, each network actor (individual, team, or organization) affects and is affected by each of the others, and each is an integral part of a larger network. In this interconnected network, we must strategically manage the time we spend improving the connections between our assets, as they affect the larger organization (Krebs, 1999).

Conclusion

Social networks enable interactive exchanges of information at tre-mendously accelerated rates. These exchanges facilitate collaborative sharing and learning, which in turn facilitates new knowledge. However, knowledge is an evolving (and often collective) matter, and the tail of learning through social networks is long and robust, beyond the capability of current measures. We are experiencing changes today that outpace anything used before to predict the speed of change.

What individuals, communities, institutions, and society generally will learn from the phenomena of social networks and the acceleration of human exchange is just beginning. The history of human interaction and communication demonstrates the extent to which value is gained, and the affect of individually identifying, examining, and sharing new knowledge for the benefit of the community.

The innovations created by our collective imaginations will implode many of the realities of today. Social networks are already pushing our thoughts to the fringe, where the tipping point of knowledge will emerge and the economics of a new era in humanity will be born: The Relation-ship Economy.

References

Carlaw, K., Oxley, L., Walker, P., Thorns, D., and Nuth, M. (2006). Beyond the Hype: Intellectual Property and the Knowledge Society/Knowledge Economy [Electronic version]. Malden, MA: Blackwell Publishing.

Charron, C., Favier, J., and Li, C. (2006). *Social Computing: How Networks Erode Institutional Power, and What to Do about It.* Forrester Customer Report, February, 2006.

Cimol, M. (Ed.). (2005). *Developing Innovation Systems: Mexico in a global context.* London: Routledge.

Grebe, Hank. Photo-Illustrations by Hank Grebe. Used with Permission, 2007.

Gurteen, D. (1999). *Creating a Knowledge Sharing Culture.* Retrieved October 15, 2007, from www.providersedge.com/docs/km_articles /Creating_a_K-Sharing_Culture_-_Gurteen.pdf http://tinyurl.com/26hbsj

Hendler, J. (2005). *Knowledge is Power: view from the Semantic Web.* Retrieved October 12, 2007, from http://www.cs.umd.edu/~hendler/presentations/engelmore.pdf

Krebs, V. (1998). *Knowledge Networks: Mapping and Measuring Knowledge Creation.* Retrieved October 12, 2007, from http://www.knetmap.com/knowledge-networks-mapping.html

Krebs, V. (1999). *Working in the Connected World: Managing Connected Assets.* Retrieved October 12, 2007, from http://www.knetmap.com/connected-assets.html

Parameswaran, M. and Whinston, A. B. (June, 2007). Research Issues in Social Computing, *Journal of the Association for Information Systems*, 8(6), 336. Retrieved October 10, 2007 from http://crec.mccombs.utexas.edu/works/articles/Parameswaran_ Social%20Computing_JAIS07.pdf http://tinyurl.com/yt6b6u

Peizer, J. (2000). Bridging The Digital Divide: First You Need The Bridge. The Media Channel, June 21, 2000. Retrieved October 10, 2007 from http://www.mediachannel.org/views/oped/peizer.shtml

Rollyson, C. S. (2006). The Knowledge Economy: The Ultimate Context for Understanding the Future. Economy: The Global Human Capital Journal, last modified 2007-1-19. Retrieved January 26, 2008 from www.globalhumancapital.org/download/Knowledge_Economy_Ultimate_Future_Context.pdf http://tinyurl.com/2ynvo2

Wang, F., Zeng, D., Carley, K. M., and Mao, W. (2007). *Social Computing: From Social Informatics to Social Intelligence,* IEEE Intelligent Systems, vol. 22, no. 2, 2007, pp. 79-83. Retrieved October 12, 2007 from http://dsonline.computer.org

Wasko, M. M. and Faraj, S. (2000). It is what one does: why people participate and help others in electronic communities of practice. *Journal of Strategic Information Systems* 9 (2000) pp. 155-173 Retrieved October 12, 2007 from www.sc-eco.univ-nantes.fr/~tvallee /memoire/pratique/why%20people%20participate.pdf http://tinyurl.com/26luae

Wittig, G. (nd). *Expansive Order: Situated and Distributed Knowledge Production in Network Space.* Retrieved October 15, 2007, from http://www.c5corp.com/research/situated_distributed.shtml

4 The Relationship Factors

Jay T. Deragon

The paradigm change we will encounter in The Relationship Economy is best summarized in the phrase, "Markets are Conversations" (Levine, Locke, Searls, and Weinberger, 2000). This phrase suggests that changes will be required from organizations as they respond to the new marketplace environment. The authors assert that the Internet is unlike the ordinary media used in mass marketing campaigns because it enables people to have "human-to-human" conversations, which have the potential to transform traditional business practices radically (Levine et al., 2000).

The biggest wedge in the social pie in The Relationship Economy is that of relationships. Customers have an influence on prices, but only in the form of aggregate demand. The rates at which they buy or do not buy something determines what price the market will bear—in a system where "market" means aggregate demand, manifested in prices paid and quantities sold. The economic system is viewed mostly through the prism of price, which is seen as the outcome of tug-of-war between supply and demand.

Sociologists are now producing studies around the dynamics of relationships and economics. Brayden King, professor of sociology at BYU writes, "One of the central themes of economic sociology is that relationships matter to market functioning." The theme is captured most succinctly with the "markets-as-networks" tag. Markets are just a special kind of network—one in which relationships facilitate trading of assets. However, sociologists are not alone in their efforts to analyze the relational aspects of markets. Economists and finance scholars are actually doing quite a bit of network research that is not being picked up by economic sociologists. For example, an article in the June 2007 issue of *The Journal of Finance*, "Reputation Effects in Trading on the New York Stock Exchange," argues that relationships between traders and brokers in the New York Stock Exchange lower trading costs. The study also demonstrates, rather nicely, that social networks help people lower the costs of doing business.

Most network studies focus on the revenue side, but the Dean of the Yale School of Management, Joel Podolny (2005), maintains that the gains associated with certain structural properties like status or reputation may be mostly due to cost cutting. High-status investment banks hire the best employees at a lower cost than their lower-status competitors. Securities specialists with good reputations have lower trading costs. If a stockbroker cuts all ties with his or her colleagues, he or she will have to begin rebuilding his or her reputation with a completely new set of traders. Thus, cutting old ties and forming new relationships is costly.

Now enter social networking mediums and the related dynamics, according to Podolny. The use of a medium creates a significant shift in one's ability to have multiple conversations, and now expanding and building relationships is no longer a costly process; in fact, it is accelerated.

Determining the Intrinsic Value of The Relationship Economy

Traditional definitions of economics drive most current theories of value. Right now, we are on the crest of expanding the definition of economics and creating a new theory for the intrinsic value of relationships.

An intrinsic theory of value in any theory of value economics holds that the value of an object, good, or service is intrinsic or contained in the item itself. Most such theories look to the process of producing an item, and the costs involved in that process, as a measure of the item's intrinsic value.

Intrinsic value, therefore, is the argument that the value of a product is inherent within the product, rather than dependent on the buyer's perception. In commodity markets, the intrinsic value of money, as a commodity, can be partially or entirely due to the desirable features of it as a medium of exchange and a store of value.

Inserting the definitions into The Relationship Economy, the intrinsic value of a relationship between two people is what we as individuals produce as value for others and society as a whole. By using networking as the medium of exchange, we are producing value, mostly for those with whom we have relationships (connections), and in many cases, for those with whom we are not "connected."

The value of the relationship is categorized into four elements of the individual, and may be of one dimension or a combination:

- Economic
- Intellectual
- Emotional
- Spiritual

The intrinsic value of relationships is the giving we provide to others for their gain. How much we give and produce for others determines the features of our relationships and the store of our value (Shuman and Twombly, 2006).

Giving is measured by the attributes of the four elements previously defined.

If we build taxonomy of value using these four elements, we can then establish measures that can be quantified by the market, which is defined as, those to whom we are connected and social networks. Those who produce the most intrinsic value are those who give the most value and contribute to the overall Relationship Economy.

Given that such a "system" could be built and measured, can you imagine the impact globally? We, the founding members of The Relationship Economy, could create a wave of value creation that appeals to the very essence of human nature, giving and gaining measurable results. The results, individually and collectively, could create a completely new economic exchange very similar to existing stock exchanges that are the foundation of the global economy.

Imagine YOU, as a brand listed on the Relationship Stock Exchange, with a price per share that is determined by the very attributes described above. Instead of producing traditional profits and losses, your brand only produces measurable gains, or losses, for others measured in the four elements previously discussed.

Considering the state of the world in which each of us lives—with war, terrorism, global unrest, and economic uncertainty, in addition to rapid change brought on by technology—we have the ability to create the wave of change based on relationships, one-to-one, then to millions.

We have the ability to "change our world," and the power of numbers can accelerate the change if we create a common vision and execute our deliverables with consideration toward moving forward with that vision. King Solomon once said, "Without vision the people perish."

When we talk about the subject matter of the creation of The Relationship Economy, we cover a series of analyses regarding the emergence of it. The new economy is facilitated by the convergence of technological mediums aimed at enabling transactions of economic value through relationships.

We can visually see the values of our relationships by using the Relationship Matrix.

     Chapter 4: The Relationship Factors

RELATIONSHIP MATRIX FACTORS

	Time Factors	Knowledge Factors	Relationship Factors	Networked Factors	Technology Factors	Economic Factors	Systemic Factors	Cultural Factors	Influence Factors	Media Factors	Gender Factors	Age Factors	Individual Factors	Relationship Capital Factors	Us Factors	Political Factors	Human Factors	Learning Factors	Industry Factors	Planning Factors	Future Factors
Time Factors																					
Knowledge Factors																					
Relationship Factors																					
Networked Factors																					
Technology Factors																					
Economic Factors																					
Systemic Factors																					
Cultural Factors																					
Influence Factors																					
Media Factors																					
Gender Factors																					
Age Factors																					
Individual Factors																					
Relationship Capital Factors																					
Us Factors																					
Political Factors																					
Human Factors																					
Learning Factors																					
Industry Factors																					
Planning Factors																					
Future Factors																					

Jay Deragon : www.linktoyourworld.com

The Relationship Matrix

The relationship matrix is used to consider one relationship factor with another as well as the subsequent value proposition aimed at producing a result. Individuals, institutions, organizations and governments within the matrix define the results. Results can also be defined by the interaction of all relationships collectively. Our initial analysis identified the first of many factors currently influencing the emergence of The Relationship Economy. Taken within a matrix, the combined factors illustrate the potential of over 400 possible interactions that both define and impact results.

Using the Relationship Matrix

The purpose of the matrix is to provide a basis for market segments of The Relationship Economy to define which factors provide the most influence to achieve a desired result. Using other management tools such as a prioritization matrix, affinity diagramming, and systemic mapping of the organization can help strategically align the organization. By using these tools, the alignment of relationships and efforts to maximize opportunities is executed with clarity of purpose and in context to achieve specific goals. The dynamics of the current "networking space" is filled with reactionary responses to the stimulus of opportunity fueled by both the hype and the adoption of users to the new medium. The most influential factor for success is the ability to leverage multiple factors within the matrix, and it is imperative to do so expeditiously.

References

Levine, R., Locke, C., Searls, D., and Weinberger, D. (2000). *The Cluetrain Manifesto: The End of Business as Usual.* New York: Perseus Books.

Podolny, J. (2005). *Status Signals: A Sociological Study of Market Competition.* Princeton, NJ: Princeton University Press.

Searls, D. (2007). Building an Relationship Economy. http://www.linuxjournal.com/node/1000182 referencing *The Cluetrain Manifesto,* Retrieved October 17, 2007, from http://cluetrain.com

Shuman, J. and Twombly, J. (2006). *Introducing Relationship Business. The Rhythm of Business, Inc.* Retrieved October 10, 2007, from www.rhythmofbusiness.com/LeadingThoughts/Relationship Overview.asp http://tinyurl.com/28vd8l

5 The Networked Factors

Scott Allen

Anthropologist Robin Dunbar (1992), through his research on primate brain size and social behavior, theorized that as primate brains evolve, they become larger in order to handle the unique complexities of larger social groups. Humans, with the largest brain size, also have the largest expected group size—about 150 people. In other words, our brains are hard-wired to handle a maximum of about 150 close relationships—people whose names and faces we remember and immediately recognize, or those we miss if we do not see them for an extended period. As Dunbar described it, these are the people you would not feel embarrassed about joining uninvited for a drink if you bumped into them at a bar (1992).

Clearly, 150 is a very low number of close connections for active business people. The typical businessperson will work closely with that many coworkers, clients, vendors, business partners, and industry colleagues within a couple of years, and many times more than that over the course of his or her career. Add to that one's close personal relationships through family, school, social, and civic activities, and it easily runs into the high hundreds or several thousand. According to a May 2007 report from social software vendor

Plaxo, "The average Plaxo address book has 203 contacts, although it is not uncommon for individuals to use Plaxo to stay in touch with several thousand contacts" (Plaxo, 2007).

Social software enhances not only our ability to build a very large network of extremely weak ties, but also our ability to push the envelope of our close ties; we want to treat more people the same way we treat the 150 that our brain can handle. Social software provides a sort of "distributed cognition" by reminding us of facts, faces, history, and other useful contextual information for our interpersonal interactions. That said, there are still functional limits, and because of the trade-offs that exist between the many factors, the challenge of figuring out ideal networking practices is not one of *maximization*, but rather one of *optimization*.

Michael Pokocky, Copyright © 2007

The Forest and the Trees

Some individuals may not realize that there is a tendency for organizations to look at forests (networks) and individuals to look at trees (individual relationships). It is important for organizational leaders to remember that networks consist of individual relationships, and that any effective strategy for leveraging social networks, whether virtual or in-person, must include strategies for creating, building, and sustaining

   Chapter 5: The Networked Factors

individual relationships. People are not just nodes on a network map, and attempts to automate relationship management that ignore this factor can be dehumanizing and sometimes backfire.

At the same time, individuals will derive more benefits from their network if they think strategically about building and sustaining their network in aggregate rather than just focusing solely on the individual relationships.

The Seven Keys to a Powerful Network

In their book, *The Virtual Handshake: Opening Doors and Closing Deals Online*, David Teten and Scott Allen introduced their "Seven Keys to a Powerful Network:"

1. **Character:** Your integrity, clarity of motives, consistency of behavior, openness, discretion, and trustworthiness. This is the real content of your character, and it is how each acquaintance perceives your character.

2. **Competence:** Your ability to walk your talk; your demonstrated capability. It includes functional knowledge and skills, interpersonal skills, and judgment. Similarly, this is driven by both the real level of your competence and the level at which acquaintances view your competence.

3. **Relevance:** The acquaintance's value to you, defined as the acquaintance's ability to contribute to your own goals. The acquaintance's relevance is driven by the value of the acquaintance's own network.

4. **Information:** The data that you have about the acquaintance. First are the basic coordinates: e-mail address, phone numbers, family information, and so on. Additional, highly valuable information includes professional background, career advancement, coworker attitudes about you, and likes and dislikes.

5. **Strength:** The closeness of the relationship between you and your acquaintance. This reflects the degree of trust and reciprocity.

6. **Number:** How many people you know directly, including both strong and weak ties.

7. **Diversity:** The heterogeneity of your network by geography, profession, industry, and hierarchical position. In addition, your network should ideally be diverse by age, sex, ethnicity, political orientation, and so on.

(Teten and Allen, 2005)

The Virtual Handshake describes these seven keys in detail, which is not duplicated here, but below are additional observations not covered in that publication.

The first and foremost issue is that while there is no practical maximum for each of these keys on its own (along whatever scale it is measured), each of them takes time to grow.

- Increasing your network's perception of your character and building stronger relationships typically requires spending time being of service to members of your network or in communities in which they also participate.

- Demonstrating your competence requires you to spend time publishing, speaking, and communicating your expertise, as well as time in professional development to maintain and grow your knowledge and skills.

- The time spent obtaining and managing information about your network grows linearly in proportion to the number of people in your network.

- Meeting people and building relationships take time, of course. Moreover, the people who are relevant to your current business objectives are typically homogenous. The people you meet who are immediately relevant are not diverse.

Because all of these keys are constrained by time, it is impossible to maximize all of them. If you have time to meet ten people, you should consider whether they are all going to be immediately relevant and homogenous, diverse, or lie somewhere in the middle. If you have an hour to spend on relationships, you should determine whether you spend it reaching several hundred or several thousand people, writing a blog post and demonstrating your competence, or reviewing one friend's manuscript and strengthening that relationship which might increase your professional competence by acquiring new knowledge.

     Chapter 5: The Networked Factors

A common misconception among many newcomers to social media and social networking is that it is all about numbers. They add as many friends as possible on social networking sites, measure the success of their blogs based on number of unique visitors, and answer as many questions as possible on forums such as on LinkedIn Answers to increase their visibility.

However, these activities all have trade-offs. A key factor in networking is the action threshold. The action threshold is the level of relationship strength that is required for the person to take action on your behalf, either reactively or proactively. Simply put, the better people know you, the more willing they are to do more for you (and you for them). If you are making a request of them, the strength required is proportional to the risk and effort involved in the task. If you want people to act on your behalf without asking, then the relationship has to be even stronger.

If the strength of a given relationship is not above the action threshold, the cost of obtaining and maintaining it, no matter how small, exceeds the value if that relationship has little potential to evolve. This is when and why it is important to look at it from the perspective of the overall network. We need to consider the value of a particular relationship. Thinking strategically affords the objectivity necessary to filter your re-lationship options; thus, you will be able to recognize and invest time in relationships that you believe will ultimately rise above the action threshold.

It is arguable that relationships you do not pursue might be potentially useful contacts in the future, but that is the point of social networking sites—you do not have to be directly connected with people in order to be able to locate and communicate with them later. The entire mem-bership of a social networking site is "potential" connections. Dion Hinchcliffe provides a depiction of the correlations between current and potential connections established by push or pull and their potential maximum value.

Network Effects
Push vs. Pull Establishment of Connections

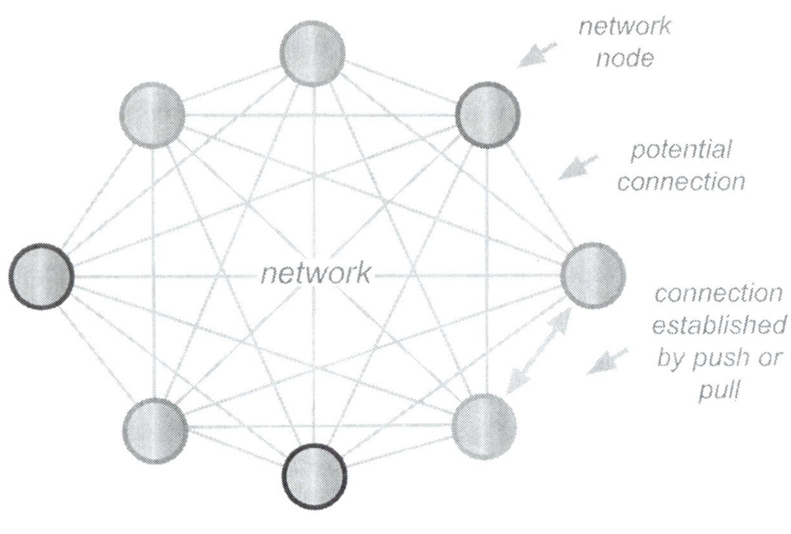

Figure 1: Network Effects (Dion Hinchcliffe, 2008)

Therefore, as stated earlier, the challenge of developing an effective strategy for social media and social networking participation is not one of maximization, but one of optimization. Each individual user will have an optimal balance of the seven keys at any given point in time, depending on his or her current objectives. Someone selling enterprise

     Chapter 5: The Networked Factors

software to Fortune 500 clients will need a small number of people but will require higher credibility and stronger relationships with them, while someone marketing information products will want to reach a large number of people with an emphasis on professional competence.

Proper use of the seven keys framework allows individuals to do something that most networking methodologies fail to do: clearly align networking activities with business objectives.

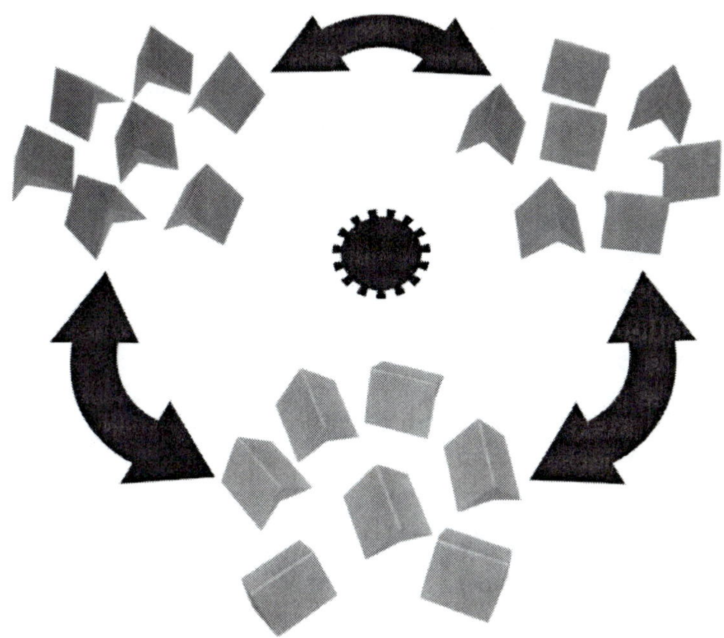

Network Topology

Contrary to popular opinion, a "closed" network is not necessarily one in which access to membership is tightly controlled, either explicitly or implicitly. A closed network is one in which everyone is so tightly connected that no member can easily avoid being noticed by others. For example, if you make a major mistake at work, odds are that most of your co-workers will know about it, but your family probably will not, unless you tell them. Each of those is a closed network and you are the bridge filling the structural hole between them.

Despite the apparent openness of networks provided by large social networking services and the advocacy of total openness by some modern networking evangelists, there are actually many advantages to closed networks, and they will continue to serve a valuable purpose. Some of the benefits of closed networks include:

1. **Information benefits:** Information deteriorates in quality as it passes through more steps. In a closed network, you have multiple ways to access the same information, which makes it more likely that you will get accurate information.

2. **Control benefits:** In a closed network, it is easier to create both positive and negative social consequences for members, which in turn builds trust among members. You are less likely to cheat your customers if they have a user group in which they share experiences and compare notes because that abuse could hurt your relationships with other customers.

3. **Relationship benefits:** A closed network typically has a stronger sense of common identity based on shared experiences and shared purpose. Being a classmate from a small high school in which everybody knew each other is usually a stronger tie than being a classmate from a large university.

Human beings have an instinctive desire to connect with others who have similar interests, in small groups. Closed networks are a healthy and natural part of our human existence.

In fact, the ability to create closed networks easily differentiates contemporary social networking sites from earlier Web-based communities. In traditional Web communities, the site creators pre-determine discussion forum categories to prevent redundancy. However, in social networking sites, anyone who wants to create a group, can do so. As a result, you might easily end up with proliferation of groups, such as an "entrepreneurs" group, a "small business" group, a "small business owners" group, a "small business issues" group, and so on, each with its own unique flavor defined by the creator of the group and evolved over time by its members.

Ideally, you become a member of many closed networks. This makes you a bridge in the structural holes between these networks within the larger network. As a bridge, you become a valuable source of information for other members of your closed networks. In some cases, being able to control that flow at your discretion may have value as well.

In *The Virtual Handshake*, the authors make the following recommendation:

> We recommend that you seek opportunities to place yourself in structural holes. For example, inter-organizational working groups, joint ventures, and industry lobbying groups are all excellent venues for you to become a new connection between groups.
>
> Filling a structural hole can be very lucrative, monetarily and in social capital. Executive recruiters, investment bankers, and other professional middle people make a healthy living bridging these holes. Even if you do not charge money for making those connections, being known as the "go-to guy" for connections to a particular group of people is highly advantageous. (Teten and Allen, 2005, p. 16)

The Network Effect

Why all of this emphasis on networks? What makes them so intriguing? In two words: exponential math.

As a concrete example, with approximately 500 direct connections on one popular social networking Web site, you will typically have access to 150,000-200,000 people at two degrees and 3-4 million people at three degrees, i.e., people who are a friend of a friend of a friend.

On the other hand, in an open system, you can post something in your blog or a discussion forum that hundreds or thousands of people will read. If the information you share is valuable, then some of them will share it with their connections. If they are bridge connectors, they may share it with other groups as well.

In practice, the network effect is rarely quite as spectacular as the raw math might suggest because of some of the constraints mentioned above. It takes time for people to relay messages, and unless the perceived value to them exceeds the time and effort cost of doing so, they will not do it.

It is important not to overtax networks. Demanding too much effort and attention from them will reduce the efficacy of the channel and eventually shut it down entirely.

Conclusion

Human beings are the constituent parts of social networks. Nevertheless, there is strategic value in looking at relationships taken together as a network. Understanding and applying both network topology and the "Seven Keys to a Powerful Network" (Teten and Allen, 2005) allows individuals to better align their networking activities with their business objectives, improve their focus, and get better results with less effort.

References

Dunbar, R.I.M. (1992). Neocortex size as a constraint on group size in primates. *Journal of Human Evolution*, 20, 469-493.

Hinchcliffe, Dion. Copyright Dion Hinchcliffe. All Rights Reserved. Used with Permission, 2008. Dion Hinchcliffe's Web 2.0 Blog. http://web2.socialcomputingmagazine.com

Plaxo press release (2007). *Talent Agents, Publicists, Politicians, and CEOs Top 'Connected Index' as Most Well-Connected Professions.* Retrieved October 2, 2007, from http://www.plaxo.com/about/releases/release-20070523

Pokocky, Michael (2007). Sketches used by permission. All rights reserved and provided with gracious permission to use by the authors of this book.

Teten, D. and Allen, S. (2005). *The Virtual Handshake: Opening Doors and Closing Deals Online.* New York: AMACOM, 2005. Available at http://thevirtualhandshake.com

6 The Technology Factors

Scott Allen

A critical factor in understanding the relationship of technology to The Relationship Economy is the fact that most users do not adopt a new technology or service directly because of the technological features. Technology attracts early adopters, and the mainstream typically follows.

Consider a case in point: the mass migration of users from Friendster to MySpace in 2004-2005. To the casual observer, Friendster and MySpace may offer similar functionality. The key difference is that the technology on MySpace enabled freedom of expression and individuality, while that of Friendster was restrictive and conforming. As such, the musicians and artists who wanted to express themselves more freely were attracted to MySpace. Once they started to move, their fans started to move, and from there it was a domino effect (Boyd, 2006).

Another critical factor is that the technology does not have to be radically innovative and enable new functionality in order to hit a tipping point and move toward widespread adoption. Often, all it takes is a better mousetrap. As communications researcher Everett Rogers (1995) discussed, one of the criteria that individuals use in their decisions to adopt a new technology is its complexity, or conversely, its simplicity. Technological advances, which result in simplified processes, spur widespread adoption.

Blogging is a prime example. Blogging software is simplified such that someone who possesses a minimal knowledge of Web design can use it. To illustrate the change this software brings about, consider the following scenario: You read something online which you want to comment on, with quotes, and share with your friends and business associates. Using pre-blogging tools, that process would take over 30 discrete steps. With blogging, it takes three.

A third critical factor is the trend toward consolidation. While there may be a large number of content and information sources available, historically there has been a significant trend towards consolidating those for the user. Email previously required users to log in separately to each email system in which they participated in order to check messages. Then came email clients that handled multiple systems through a common interface. Blogs were first read as Web sites (and many still do), but the advent of RSS readers allowed users to consolidate everything to a common inbox. While they may visit the Web site to read the full content, the RSS reader provides a single tool for first-pass information filtering.

With these factors in mind, the following are the major technology trends we see with regard to The Relationship Economy. All of these technologies currently exist, but most are in the very early stages and have not yet seen widespread mainstream adoption.

Identity Management

One of the most significant barriers to participating in any new virtual community is the time it takes to set up a robust profile and re-establish relationship data. For several years, the "holy grail" of identity management has been to have a unified or federated identity system, which would allow single sign-on between multiple systems. However, competitive concerns and technological complexity have prevented the widespread adoption of such a solution.

There are a substantial number of competing standards in this area, but it has become clear that a single widely accepted standard is unlikely to occur any time soon. Currently, the trend is toward a federated approach—using standards-based protocols to enable one application to assert the identity of a user to another, thereby avoiding the need for redundant authentication. The two most promising technologies in this area are SAML, the open standard developed by OASIS and the Liberty Alliance, and WS-Federation, co-developed by BEA Systems, BMC Software, CA, Inc., IBM, Layer 7 Technologies, Microsoft, Novell, and VeriSign.

We estimate that widespread adoption of these federated authentication mechanisms is still three to five years away. In the meantime, business opportunities exist for services that simplify identity management from the user's perspective. If a user is willing to provide his or her user ID and password to a third party aggregator service, that service can then log in to multiple services as the user and manage the user's profile and relationship information from a single interface.

Current players in this space include:
- 8hands
- iStalkr
- Minggl
- MyLifeBrand
- Naymz
- PeopleAggregator
- Profilactic
- ProfileFly
- ProfileLinker

- ProfileOmat
- Second Brain
- Snag
- Socialnetwork.in
- Socialstream
- SocialURL
- Spokeo
- Tabber
- UpScoop

Content and Data Syndication

Another significant time drain on the individual participant in social software is the matter of content syndication. Copy/paste sounds simple enough, but if you are writing several pieces of content daily and participating in multiple sites, that becomes both a cost- and time-prohibitive task. RSS is meant to address this, but while the use of RSS has become widespread, there are still several needs not well met by the current technologies.

For example, how can the typical user display RSS-sourced content from their external blog in their social networking profile? Historically, there has been no way to embed server-side code and while there are Javascript and Flash-based solutions, most sites do not allow Javascript and many (particularly business-oriented sites) do not allow Flash. However, new technologies such as Facebook's API (Application Programming Interface) and Google's OpenSocial initiative are rapidly changing this. What about displaying that content in the sidebar of the blog? Code for it is readily available, but it is still not "blog-simple" for the non-technical user.

Moreover, what about more interactive applications, such as calendars, task lists, contact management and so on? Currently, the most common solution in this area is Flash widgets. Widgetbox.com offers the largest directory of widgets available, as well as allowing users to configure and manage widgets for specific applications or content sources. SpringWidgets is one of the most innovative players in the space, offering a widget development platform for both Web and desktop.

While widgets offer an interim solution, they are not the ideal long-term solution. The requirement for Flash limits their portability, as well as their display flexibility. The more robust solution is for sites to offer an open Application Programming Interface (API). At a minimum, an API allows developers to create applications for accessing a site's data and primary functionality. A more robust API will allow developers to create embedded applications for use within the site.

One of the most prominent examples of the potential for an open API is Facebook, which made their API public in August 2006. As of February 2008, there are more than 15,000 embedded applications available within Facebook. Another major innovator in the API space is Ning, an application that allows users to build their own social networks for free (or private-label them for a small fee). The success of Facebook's API program has sent other networking sites scrambling, with most of the major players making some kind of announcement at least hinting at an API of their own.

In light of the fact that APIs are much easier to build in than to add on, it is our strong recommendation that any new offering in the social software space at this point must include an API at the time of launch in order to gain traction.

Enterprise Integration

The factors mentioned above are required first steps toward enterprise integration. Social network tools that focus on the enterprise, such as Spoke Software, Leverage Software, Visible Path, and Contact Network Corporation, have built their applications with enterprise integration in mind. However, they have not garnered the widespread consumer and small business adoption that certain public networks, such as LinkedIn and Facebook have garnered. Although consumers, potential employees, and small business partners will not be easily reached on a large scale through closed network systems (such as those mentioned above), this does not diminish the value of those tools—they just do not reach the open marketplace as effectively.

We expect to see a trend in enterprise integration, and it could come from either of two sources: the enterprise network vendors who are developing integrations with the public networks as they make APIs available, or from the public networking sites making integrations available with other enterprise systems such as CRM and enterprise portals.

User Data Ownership

In the industry analysis of social networking services, there is much talk regarding the intrinsic value of the user's data. Sites have been reluctant to open up access to their data because they realize it is a core asset.

The reality, though, is that users own their data—users own the content they produce. As part of the user agreement, they may grant the site certain rights, such as the ability to use content for promotional purposes, but users can easily take their data away and move it to another service with relative ease. The only thing generally preventing it is the time-consuming aspect, which becomes even more daunting the more heavily vested a user becomes in a particular site.

As the money involved in the social networking space becomes more and more visible in the news, users are starting to wonder a) where their share of that revenue is, and b) whether they want to entrust ownership of their data to a third-party service, particularly one from which they are unable to easily retrieve it.

This is creating two important trends: revenue sharing and open data.

Revenue Sharing

A growing number of services are offering various forms of revenue sharing with content producers, and in some cases active users who are not content producers. A variety of models exist, including the insertion of the user's Google Adsense codes in pages they create, points and rewards systems for user participation, and direct compensation for page views or for recruiting members. Another interesting new direction coming to the forefront is the enablement of ad insertions into audio and video, which allows members to earn ad revenue regardless of where they post their media.

                                    Chapter 6: The Technology Factors

Open Data

The profile aggregators mentioned above still have one fundamental problem: While they simplify data entry and maintenance, the user's data is still stored in a third-party proprietary system.

A solution to this and one of the most interesting social networking concepts is SocialGrid. SocialGrid is a social networking site, but the data is stored on the user's own site as metadata using an open standard (users can store their data on SocialGrid if they do not have their own site). Structured searches are performed using public search engines against the metadata.

A more complex problem is the portability of relationship data. There is not a single "social graph" in existence that is comprehensive, decentralized, and non-proprietary. There are, however, XML standards that would support it, and an informal working group has started collaborating on the issue.

Web Conferencing/Real-time Collaboration

Web conferencing has been around since the late 1990's and in widespread use for the past few years. However, it has still not experienced the kind of ultra-low-cost or even zero-cost disruption that Skype brought to voice communications or services such as FreeConference.com and FreeConferenceCall.com brought to voice conferencing. There are a relatively small number of companies that have sufficient need to cost-justify purchasing unlimited usage, and at the going rates of $0.25-$0.50 per minute per user, routine daily usage is cost-prohibitive.

There are vendors moving into this space, but they do not have much traction yet. Some promising newcomers at a disruptively low price point include Unite (which runs on top of Skype), Talking Communities, VoxWire and WebTrain. For those willing to install software on their own server, Teamslide and DimDim (open source) offer inexpensive alternatives. Another particularly interesting development in this space is Ojeez, a business-networking site that offers its users Web conferencing as part of its premium service package for less than $10 a month.

Software Agents

As individuals and companies become engaged in The Relationship Economy, the challenge gradually shifts from that of finding opportunity to filtering it. There are well over a billion people online to meet—more than 17 million businesspeople on LinkedIn alone. There are terabytes upon terabytes of social media content available. While it is not difficult to find people to meet, blogs to read, or discussions to participate in, it is difficult to find highly relevant people, content, and conversations.

Intelligent agents are highly customizable search routines that execute across multiple data sources and deliver search results to one of the user's existing inboxes, e.g., email or RSS. The various blog search engines all provide the ability to subscribe to search results via RSS. The challenge is searching other content sources, such as private discussion forums, groups within social networking sites, and in particular, networking profiles. These present special challenges because an individual search typically needs to be more structured, e.g., "find people in my city who used to work for XYZ Company as a manager or higher." Simple text search functions do not accommodate this specificity.

What we envision, as an example, are social networking software agents that, based on easily defined parameters, could provide a daily list of recommended new people to meet, existing contacts with whom to confer, blog posts to read, and forum discussions in which to participate. Such tools would allow both individual and corporate users to realize a dramatic increase in productivity in the use of social software. While such tools are beginning to appear within enterprise portals, there is not yet a consumer version that is functional across multiple sites available. We believe that this represents an excellent opportunity for the first movers in the space.

Conclusion

The recent surge in popularity of social media and social networking has created a wealth of opportunity and a renewed interest in the importance of one-to-one relationships not merely for the sake of the relationship alone, but for the purpose of accomplishment—be it personal goals, career development, or business objectives. A wide array of tools now exists to provide entirely new functionality in a social context—shared calendars, shared task lists, shared life goals, shared media, and so on.

Ironically, while the tools themselves are simple, the management of activities and identity across multiple services has created its own complexity. The primary technological challenge and related opportunity right now, particularly for business users, is in helping users manage this complexity and enabling users to be productive in leveraging their relationships to accomplish their personal and business objectives.

References

Boyd, D. (2006, March 21). *Friendster lost steam. Is MySpace just a fad?* Retrieved October 5, 2007, from http://www.danah.org/papers/FriendsterMySpaceEssay.html

Rogers, E. (1995). *Diffusion of Innovations*. New York: Free Press.

7 The Economic Factors

Jay T. Deragon

In The Relationship Economy, gain is driven by the value of our relationships and by the quality of our transactions. The "system" with which we build relationship capital creates economic rewards that come in many different forms. As The Relationship Economy matures, finding opportunities to achieve monetary gain will be limited to those who understand these core factors that create value—the quality and quantity of relationships formed in the social networking space, and the mediums used to facilitate those relationships.

When considering the future implications of social networking it is evident that collaborative technologies, such as platforms and software, will converge to form custom-designed personal network portals, which will provide enhanced capabilities for both personal and professional purposes. The benefits of a virtual work environment have already been illustrated and provided, yet future technological enhancements will accelerate these benefits for all parties—individuals, companies, governments, and organizations.

RELATIONSHIP ECONOMICS – WITH WHOM & WHAT

RELATIONSHIP ECONOMICS	Relationship Economic Transactions												
	Self	Family	Friends	Business	Legal	Financial	Educational	Media	Machines/Technology	Environment	Religion	Society	Other
Self													
Family													
Friends													
Business													
Legal													
Financial													
Educational													
Media													
Machines/Technology													
Environment													
Religion													
Society													
Other													

Relationship Economic Transactional Indicators:
● Strong   ○ Moderate   △ Weak

According to WorldCom's "Meetings in America III: A Study of the Virtual Workforce in 2001":

> The number one reason professionals want to participate in virtual teams more frequently is simple: increased productivity. For example, as the size of the virtual workforce in America today is growing, so is the likely impact on productivity and profitability for organizations. More than 90 percent of those surveyed agree (35% agree and 56% strongly agree) that virtual meetings save time and money. (Meetings, 2001)

Chapter 7: The Economic Factors

In addition, Dr. Jaclyn Kostner, author of *Virtual Leadership* (1994), concurs that individuals are learning how to leverage virtual networks and association.

Consider what we have at our disposal today:

- Unprecedented access to information and people.

- Technological communications tools that enable a virtual presence, including audio, video and text.

- Collaborative tools for virtual group dynamics and exchanges of information and knowledge.

- Mobile lifestyles exploding with integrated applications for virtually all things we need for working.

- Social networks that enable a reach to resources and richness in terms of content and exchanges.

Now consider the personal stresses and collective cost of today's work environments:

- Individual fuel and repair cost of commuting and the related environmental cost.

- Stress of time spent commuting to and from work, as well as time away from family.

- Personal cost for eating out, dry cleaning, parking, etc.

- Office cost for employers.

- The cost of employment fatigue and burn-out syndrome on the job.

Various studies on issues and outcomes of virtual work environments over the last several years reflect that telecommuting and remote management of geographically dispersed employees improve job satisfaction, save costs, and boost corporate productivity. Additional discoveries:

- More than two-thirds of American workers surveyed have engaged in virtual work.

- Nearly half of the workers (46%) are involved in virtual work at least once a week; 14% do so daily.

- Thirty-one (31%) of those surveyed work in a virtual management structure, i.e., their immediate manager or staff members are not located in the same office.

- Twenty-seven (27%) work for organizations with formal policies that encourage virtual work.

- Nearly half (48%) work for organizations that allow virtual work practices, even if no formal policy exists.

- The vast majority (91%) agree that virtual work saves his or her company time and money. (Meetings, 2001)

The virtual workplace will become more commonplace, as more adults become familiar with the benefits of social networking for economic rather than personal gains.

In business, we are hired based on what we know and whom we know. What you know is based on your past experiences and education. Whom we know is based on relationships, past, present, and future.

- Joining networks introduces us to relationships that reinforce or influence our values and beliefs. As we participate in networks, we learn from, and are shaped by our virtual experiences. In the physical world, our relationships—with friends, society, jobs and family—expand as we grow. Some people learn through the process of developing relationships, while some repeat what they have learned and fail to grow.

	Chapter 7: The Economic Factors

- In the virtual world, our relationships grow through participation. Some of us learn through the process and some try to force what they learned in the physical world onto the virtual world.

- In the virtual world, we strive for presence and self-improvement—economic, physical, intellectual, political, spiritual, and emotional.

- As we strive to gain more, we tend to repeat the experiences of the past and not gain, or we learn to change, and subsequently, gain more.

Now move to the framework of The Relationship Economy. Your personal networking portal removes the intermediary from your news source, and you are the distribution channel for products and services with which you have an affinity and will endorse. The advertisers will be chasing those individuals whose personal network portal shows his or her profile, traffic, and reach. Advertisers will pay premium dollars to get their products listed and endorsed on such personal networks.

Many of us currently sell products and services in exchange for economic value. The future of The Relationship Economy will be based on "value taken vs. value given." In a world connected to everything everywhere, we as individuals have the ability to profile and exchange our value and our values. Already in today's market, we are seeing an exchange of value in terms of relationship introductions and the process of using the means for job recruitment. Job recruiters make money from placements, an old model of exchange for value that human resource departments have adopted as a better method to internal staffing and screening. Now we will combine the old models of value exchange with a new one.

In the new model of the "networked world," we buy tokens of economic value. When someone provides us value, it is assumed and expected, but not written in contract form, that the receiver would reward us according to the perceptions of our value to him or her. The receiver would simply credit our token account with a value they deem appropriate for the benefit gained. In turn, we would do the same for those that deliver us value.

Because the technology of the networked world provides us with the luxury of efficiency and effectiveness, we are able to produce value to the degree we choose; some will work overtime because others will compensate them for their ability to produce, while others will receive and not compensate. The latter will be identified quickly as takers, not givers, and the entire network will know the difference. The global exchange of value ignites competitive propositions, but the rewards provided are an individual choice, not unlike today's market of products and services. Deliver value and you gain customers; deliver defects and you lose them.

The Relationship Economy will create new mediums, new measures, and accelerated exchanges that will displace traditional mediums and totally disrupt and displace existing paradigms. A new world order, which is driven by value exchanges and relationships, will emerge, and humanity will learn to adapt or lose. Those companies and individuals that do not adapt and create value will be identified and set apart from the larger network very quickly. Value migration will build momentum and create economic significance, individually and collectively.

References

Kostner, J. (1994). *Virtual Leadership*. New York: Warner Books.

Meetings in America III: A Study of the Virtual Workforce in 2001 (2001). Retrieved October 15, 2007, from http://www.effectivemeetings.com/technology/virtualteam/mci10.asp

8 The Systemic Factors

Jay T. Deragon

The Relationship Economy will require transformation of knowledge, management, media, technology, and individual participation. The prevailing cultures that are driving all business must undergo transformation.

The inner "system" of relationship networks cannot be understood without context. The transformation to The Relationship Economy requires an outside view and understanding of systems and relationships. There are two individuals who have developed long-standing principles in this area: Peter Senge and W. Edwards Deming. One of the well-known theories for systemic thinking was developed by Senge. In addition, The Deming System of Profound Knowledge arose which provides a map of theory by which to understand the dynamics of a networked world (Deming, 1986).

Profound knowledge in the world of social network mediums is the never-ending process of learning the dynamics and applying the learning to new theories of knowledge. It is gained from awareness, observation, and interactions created by new mediums that are constantly produced in a networked world. The first step is transformation of the individual (Deming, 1986).

Figure 2: LINKED: The New Science of Networks
(Barabási, 2002)

Unlike previous transformations that started at the top, this transformation is starting at the bottom, one-to-one individually, then to millions. Leadership from the bottom ensures massive adoption and fuels changes at the top. This transformation is already underway and is extensive. It comes from understanding and adoption of a new system that includes processes, dynamics, and technology, and is driven by the four parts of profound knowledge—systemic thinking, understanding variation, psychology, and use of data.

As individuals understand the new system of profound knowledge, they will be transformed and will apply new meaning and its principles to their lives, events, abilities, and interactions with people. Profound knowledge will provide individuals with the confidence in their judgment of their own decisions and in their ability to participate in the transformation of the organizations, institutions, governments, and communities to which they belong.

When an individual begins to understand the system, he or she can contribute to the body of knowledge for the masses to learn from and apply, including:

1. Setting an example of participation in the networked world.

2. Learning the dynamics and assumed rules and roles of a networked world.

3. Continually teaching others how to succeed in the networked world.

4. Helping people, organizations, institutions, and governments to pull away from their current practices and beliefs and move into the new system without reservations about past actions.

The precepts of profound knowledge listed below are interrelated and have an impact on an individual's contribution:

1. Appreciation for a system of relationship networks.

2. Knowledge about variation of networks and their subsequent value.

3. Theory of knowledge, i.e., what is being discovered and applied as the basis for future advancement of the networked world.

4. Psychology of how people relate and accomplish individual objectives in a network.

While most individuals would not label life as a "system of profound knowledge," they can intuitively identify with the core elements of this system, which draws on the tenets of human behavior and lessons learned from life experiences. Individuals do not need to be particularly proficient in each of these four precepts in order to understand the system and apply it.

Social networking is viewed as problematic and disruptive for many people in traditional business circles. They cannot, or will not, see the dynamics unfolding before their eyes. Awareness of networks and networked organizations has reached the mainstream of the business-publishing world, as evidenced in the increasing number of articles in publications such as the *Harvard Business Review* and the *Sloan Management Review.*

Many graduate business school programs now teach social network analysis and network theory. Networks exist outside of corporations as well—everyone participates in multiple networks, including the informal family, community, work, and their purely social networks of friends. Then the online social networking phenomenon explodes and traditionalists are attempting to frame it into how they see things, not how things really are.

The growth of social computing is radically changing old paradigms of media and influence whose reach is disrupting business models and market dynamics. The dynamics of change will accelerate with every new technical innovation to the medium of social networks, thus further empowering the individual to become the major influence over the masses vs. the traditional media.

The horizontal flow, citizen-to-citizen, is as real and consequential as the vertical one. The "former audience" is noted American technology writer Dan Gillmor's term for us. It refers to the owners and operators of tools that were once exclusively used by media people to capture and hold our attention.

Jay Rosen, Associate Professor and former chair, New York University's Department of Journalism writes, "The people formerly known as the audience wish to inform media people of our existence, and of a shift in power that goes with the platform shift you've all heard about" (2006). He further defines such people as "…those who were on the receiving end of a media system that ran one way, in a broadcasting pattern, with high entry fees and a few firms competing to speak very loudly while the rest of the population listened in isolation from one another—and who today are not in a situation like that at all" (2006).

In categorizing the use of blogs, Rosen refers to the mechanical printing press as the predecessor to blogs. "Once they were your printing presses; now that humble device, the blog, has given the press to us. That is why blogs have been called little First Amendment machines. They extend freedom of the press to more actors. Once it was your radio station, broadcasting on your frequency" (2006).

"Now that brilliant invention, podcasting, gives radio to us. And we have found more uses for it than we ever did. Shooting, editing and distributing video once belonged to them, Big Media. Only they could afford to reach a TV audience built in their own image. Now video is coming into the user's hands, and audience-building by former members of the audience is alive and well on the Web" (Rosen, 2006).

"We were once (exclusively) the editors of the news, choosing what ran on the front page. Now we can edit the news, and our choices send items to our own front pages. A highly centralized media system had connected people *up* to big social agencies and centers of power but not *across* to each other" (Rosen, 2006).

Jeff Jarvis (2004), a former media executive, says, "Give the people control of media, they will use it. The corollary: Do not give the people control of media, and you will lose. Whenever citizens can exercise control, they will."

Tom Curley, CEO of the Associated Press, has explained this to his people: "The users are deciding what the point of their engagement will be—what application, what device, what time, what place." We graduate from wanting media when we want it, to wanting it without the filler, to wanting media to be significantly better than it is, to publishing and broadcasting ourselves when it meets a need or sounds like fun (Stokes, 2003).

Mark Thompson, Director-General of the BBC, has a term for us: The Active Audience ("who doesn't want to just sit there but to take part, debate, create, communicate, and share") (Rosen, 2006). Another influential person in the space, Rupert Murdoch, says, "They want control over their media, instead of being controlled by it" (Speech, 2005).

The audience has been considered by those working in the media as "eyeballs." This is evidenced by John Fithian, President of the National Association of Theater Owners in the U.S who stated, "There is always a new challenge coming along for the eyeballs of our customers." (cited in Lyman, 2001).

Hank Grebe, 2007

Fithian, Ann Kirschner (entrepreneur and academic), and others who speak to the subject of the audience and its impact on media should know that operators had an exaggerated sense of their own power and mastery over others, which was the historical product of a media system that gave its power not to the audience but to the media operators. New media is undoing the power struggle of the past. Some operators involved in networking are building their own media, their own network, and many see things as they are while waiting for others to see the same.

    Chapter 8: The Systemic Factors

Media operators do not own the eyeballs. The public—formerly known as the audience—are now more visible, less fictional, more able, and less predictable. Regardless of their apparent aversion to change, media management is nonetheless faced with a transformation and should welcome this transformation and change. Nevertheless, Rosen hit the issues spot on. He sees the dynamics as they are and not the way they were.

Transition and transformation occurs from generation to generation, as well. Anais Nin said, "Each friend represents a world in us, a world possibly not born until they arrive, and it is only by this meeting that a new world is born."

The Systemic Factors emerging on the landscape are best categorized as:

1. Enablement of individuals to create, distribute and monetize content.

2. Connectivity of people, processes and economic exchanges.

3. Disruptive technological advances that accelerate social, political, organizational and economic change.

4. Constant change and discovery of how the new media both creates new models and destroys old ones.

The Relationship Economy will emerge from those who see things as they are—and can be—versus where they were. Maintaining a view of the market as a system, and understanding what are the inter-connected factors influencing systemic outcomes is the starting point of a process, resulting in economic gains.

References

Barabási, Albert-László. *LINKED: The New Science of Networks.* Perseus Publications, 2002. Cover Image Used with Permission.

Deming, W. E. (1986). *Out of the Crisis.* Cambridge, MA: MIT Press.

Grebe, Hank. Photo-Illustrations by Hank Grebe. Used with Permission, 2007.

Jarvis, J. (2004, November 11). *Argue with me.* Retrieved October 18, 2007, from http://www.buzzmachine.com/archives/2004_11_11.html#008464

Lyman, R. (2001, March 12). MEDIA; A Partly Cloudy Forecast for Theater Owners. New York Times. Retrieved October 17, 2007, from http://query.nytimes.com/gst/fullpage.html?res=9E0CE5DD133AF93 1A25750C0A9679C8B63 http://tinyurl.com/yrmtr9

Rosen, J. (2006, June 27). The People Formerly Known as the Audience. *Press Think.* Retrieved October 15, 2007, from www.journalism.nyu.edu/pubzone/weblogs/pressthink/2006/06/27/ ppl_frmr.html http://tinyurl.com/nh5oc

Senge, P. M. (2006). *The Fifth Discipline: The Art & Practice of The Learning Organisation* (2nd ed.). Australia: Random House.

Speech by Rupert Murdoch to the American Society of Newspaper Editors (2005, April 13). Retrieved October 18, 2007, from http://www.newscorp.com/news/news_247.html

Stokes, J. (2003, March 28). *Tom Curley, president and publisher of USA Today, named AP CEO to succeed Louis D. Boccardi.* Retrieved October 18, 2007, from http://www.ap.org/pages/about/pressreleases/pr_32803.html

9 The Cultural Factors

Matthew Hodgson*

The Internet is a pervasive communications medium. In the last decade alone, this medium has facilitated a level of interpersonal interaction that has not been seen in the last ten thousand years of human social evolution. It is a medium like no other, enabling people from different cultures around the globe to communicate with one another, share information, and build commercial or interest-based relationships and personal friendships (Cummings, Butler, and Kraut, 2002; Preece and Maloney-Krichmar, 2005).

Today, out of nearly 6.5 billion people on the planet, over 1 billion people use the Internet (Internet Usage, 2007), and approximately half of these visit Web sites that facilitate social interaction and networking (Ipsos Insight, 2007).

---

* *Matthew Hodgson is the Regional-Lead for Web and Information Management with SMS Management & Technology Limited, Canberra, Australia.*

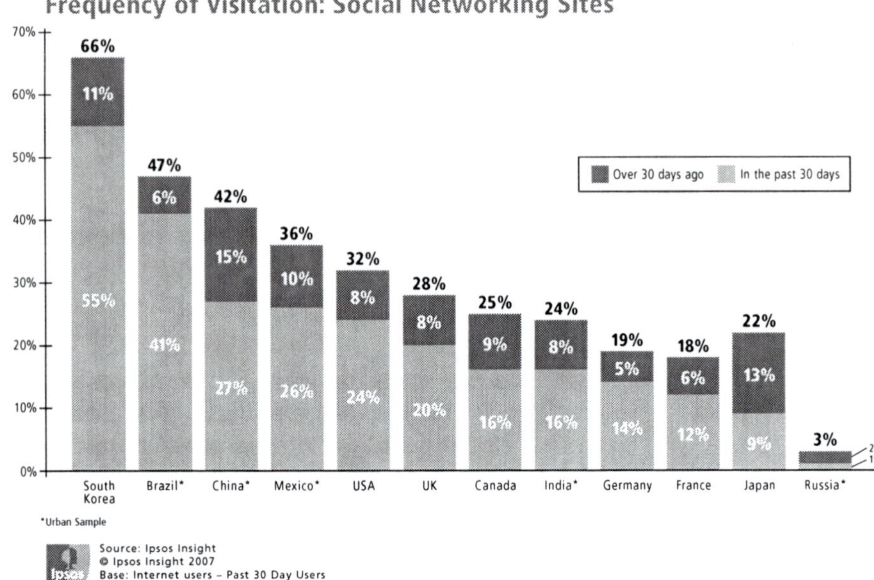

Figure 3: Frequency of Visitation: Social Networking Sites (Ipsos, 2007)

Online activity involves millions of us from cultures across the globe. Whether at play or work, people from many different cultures maintain their professional connections through LinkedIn, collaborate through MySpace, share multimedia by using YouTube, form virtual networks and communities of practice in Facebook, send short messages to each other through Twitter, and contribute to thinking and global knowledge through media ranging from personal blogs to Wikipedia.

The desire to connect with others through social networking sites is a pan-cultural trend. Data from both the blogsphere, as measured by Technorati and Wikipedia, shows significant participation by a diverse range of cultures. While the global growth in this media, for example in blogging, continues to double from year-to-year, the cultures represented by Technorati's top ten languages list as shown in Table 1 has remained relatively constant. (Sifry, 2006).

    Chapter 9: The Cultural Factors

Table 1: Technorati 2005-2007 Statistics on Blog Posts by Language

Country	Q4 2005	Q2 2006	Q3 2006	Q4 2006
Chinese	25%	12%	10%	8%
Dutch	1%	1%	0%	0%
English	25%	38%	39%	36%
French	2%	2%	2%	2%
German	1%	1%	1%	1%
Italian	3%	2%	2%	3%
Japanese	31%	32%	33%	37%
Portuguese	3%	2%	2%	2%
Russian	0%	2%	2%	2%
Spanish	4%	3%	3%	3%
Other	5%	5%	6%	6%

It is obvious that such activity occurs on a truly global scale, and aspects of our physical culture may influence the decisions that guide our adoption and interaction behavior in the virtual world.

Socioeconomic factors—education, employment, income, health—contribute to Internet usage (Taylor, Zhu, Dekkers, and Marshall, 2003). When countries are categorized according to their status of economic development (United Nations, 2005), so as to separate the effect of socioeconomic factors, other factors that contribute to the adoption of social networking can then begin to emerge.

As access to high-speed Internet increases, adoption of social net-working tools occurs faster in developing countries than in developed countries. This suggests that there are other factors at play, perhaps at a cultural level between countries, which differentiate usage behavior.

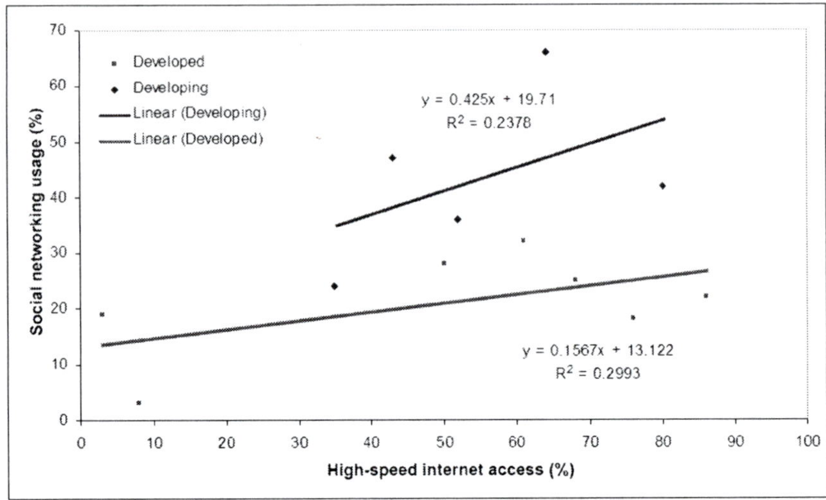

Figure 4: Social Networking Usage Against High-Speed Internet Access for Developing and Developed Countries

The term culture is difficult to define because it encompasses many things. It includes behavior, both observed and implied, that is acquired, shared, and adopted by others (Kroeber and Kluckhohn, 1952) through social learning (Bandura, 1977), and exhibited through symbolism, art, science, and even religion (Hofstede, 2005).

Geert Hofstede is a noted Dutch author on national and organizational culture. For nearly three decades, Hofstede's 1980 work on cultural dimensions has formed the basis for quantifying these aspects of culture (Hofstede, 1991). His work is also highly relevant to Web design (Marcus and Gould, 2000; Robbins and Stylianou, 2002) and aspects of Web-based communication (Tsikriktsis, 2002; Wilson, et al., 2002), making it ideal for assessment of social behavior online.

With regard to social relationships, Basabe and Ros (2005) suggest that Individualism/Collectivism and Power-Distance are the two most important dimensions for differentiating nations and cultures.

     Chapter 9: The Cultural Factors

Hofstede (2003) defines these two cultural dimensions in the following ways:

a. **"Individualism/Collectivism:** Represent the degree to which individuals are integrated into groups. On the individualist side, we find societies in which the ties between individuals are loose: everyone is expected to look after himself or herself and his or her immediate family. On the collectivist side, we find societies in which people from birth onwards are integrated into strong, cohesive in-groups, often extended families (with uncles, aunts and grandparents) which continue protecting them in exchange for unquestioning loyalty. The word 'collectivism' in this sense has no political meaning: it refers to the group, not to the state. Again, the issue addressed by this dimension is an extremely fundamental one, regarding all societies in the world."

b. **"Power-Distance:** The extent to which the less powerful members of organizations and institutions (like the family) accept and expect that power is distributed unequally. This represents inequality (more versus less), but defined from below, not from above. It suggests that a society's level of inequality is endorsed by the followers as much as by the leaders. Power and inequality, of course, are extremely fundamental facts of any society and anybody with some international experience will be aware that 'all societies are unequal, but some are more unequal than others.'"

Basabe and Ros (2005) add that Hofstede's Individualism dimension refers to the relative priority given to the person or the group (often the extended family). A meta-analysis by Oyserman, Coon, and Kemmelmeier (2002) shows that core aspects of individualist beliefs are:

- Personal independence

- Uniqueness

- Competition

- Personal achievement and success

- Introspection

- Emphasis on internal attributes rather than other people's opinions and indications

Hofstede typically describes cultures with low Individualism scores as Collectivist. These cultures do not encourage focusing attention on the inner self, and they believe the most salient features of emotional experience are external. Hui and Triandis (1986) describe the core aspects of collectivist cultural beliefs as:

- Feeling of involvement in, and contribution to, the lives of others

- Sharing of material benefits

- Sharing of nonmaterial resources

- Willingness of the person to accept the opinions and views of others

- Concern by a person about the effects of actions or decisions on others

- Concern about self-presentation

- Belief in the correspondence of own outcomes with the outcomes of others

Because social interaction focuses on the group dynamic and at a group level focuses on sharing and is less concerned with personal independence, personal achievement, and competition, it can be expected that those cultures low on Hofstede's Individualism Index will use social network Web sites more than those cultures high on the Individualism Index.

In high Power-Distance cultures, an important emotional distance separates subordinates from authorities. Respect and formal deference for higher status people (e.g., parents, elders, and even government officials) are valued. The Power-Distance dimension relates to the way power is organized in society in general, including differential rewards between high and low status people. Basabe and Ros (2005, p. 190) refer to low Power-Distance scores as "egalitarian." This suggests that egalitarian countries like Finland, Sweden, Denmark, Iceland, Australia, Netherlands, and Canada (Kragh and Bislev, 2004) can score high on Individualism while still believing strongly in the collective good and work collectively. With respect to use of social network Web sites, low

Power-Distance cultures (i.e., high levels of egality) are therefore expected to have higher usage than high Power-Distance cultures.

To investigate the nuances of meaning within Hofstede's Individualism and Power-Distance, Basabe and Ros (2005) correlated the two factors against similar measures within the cross-cultural psychology literature as shown in Table 2. Again, this shows that egalitarianism is highly correlated with Individualism and negatively correlated with Power-Distance.

Table 2: Correlations between Hofstede's Definitions and Other Cultural Factors (Basabe and Ross, 2005)

	Individualism (Hofstede)	**Power-Distance (Hofstede)**
Conservatism (Schwartz)	-.44*	.37*
Hierarchy (Schwartz)	-.44*	.21
Affective Autonomy (Schwartz)	.35*	-.50*
Intellectual Autonomy (Schwartz)	.36*	-.30#
Egalitarian Commitment (Schwartz)	.46*	-.35*
Egalitarian Commitment (Trompenaars)	.54*	-.58*
Utilitarian Involvement (Trompenaars)	.42*	-.14
Post-materialism (Inglehart)	.64*	-.60*

Note: Pearson product-moment coefficients across nations. A high number on each variable denotes a high score on the variable in question.

* p ≤. 05 (two-tailed) #p ≤.10 (two-tailed).

Using status of economic development (UNCTAD Handbook of Statistics, 2007) as the primary differentiator, significant correlations result when examining cultures on Individualism-Collectivism and Power-Distance scales.

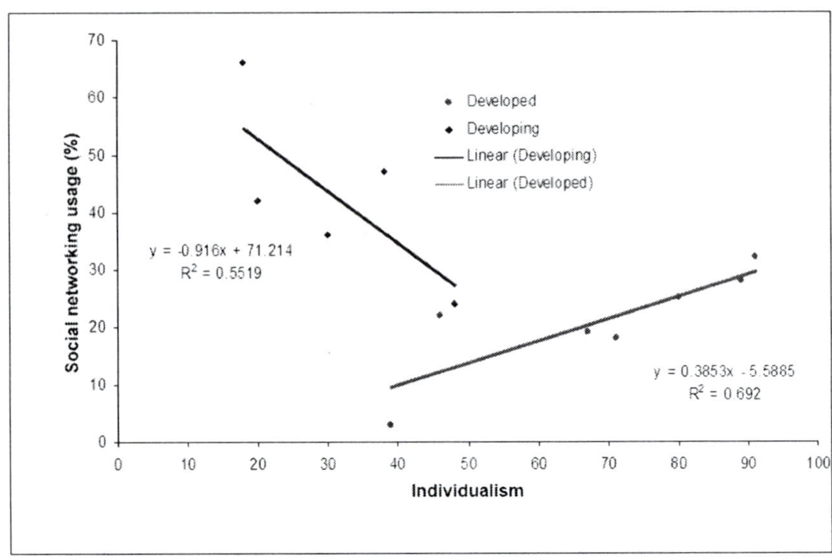

Figure 5: Social Networking Usage and Individualism for Developing and Developed Countries

Overall, Collectivist developing countries usage of social networking sites is greater than that of Individualist developed countries: a result that is consistent with Hofstede's definitions and his cultural dimensions index.

Developing countries who are less Individualist are more likely to use social networking Web sites ($y = -0.916x + 71.214$, $R^2 = 0.5519$). In contrast, in developed countries those who are more Individualist are more likely to use social networking Web sites ($y = 0.3853x - 5.5885$, $R^2 = 0.692$).

Certain studies show that both France and Germany have relatively low adoption of social networking sites. Given that each country has a score of approximately 70 on Individualism, Kemp *et al.*'s (2007) research is confirmed by the preceding figure.

  Chapter 9: The Cultural Factors

A possible reason for the opposite effect seen in Individualism is the interaction with Schwartz's (1994) Egalitarian Commitment factors, both of which are positively correlated with Hofstede's Individualism dimension. It may also be the result of another factor: Power-Distance.

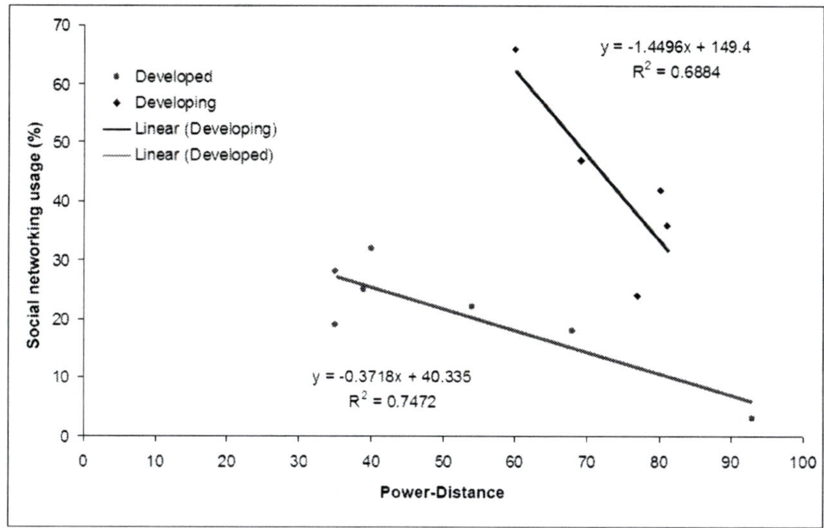

Figure 6: Social Networking Usage and Power-Distance for Developing and Developed Countries

When investigating Power-Distance, the results reflect an overall trend: as Power-Distance increases, use of social networking sites decreases. This is consistent with Hofstede's definition when taking Basabe and Ros' (2005) comments on egality into consideration.

For developing countries, those who are relatively low on Power-Distance (e.g., Korea) are more likely to use social networking sites than those who are relatively high on Power-Distance (e.g., Mexico and China) ($y = -1.4496x + 149.4$, $R^2 = 0.6884$).

Developed countries show a similar relationship, with Power-Distance having a strong effect on use of social networking sites ($y = -0.3718x + 40.335$, $R^2 = 0.7472$).

Overall, these results show that all cultures use social networking sites, but that Collectivist cultures' participation is higher overall than Individualist cultures. This is to be expected, given the collectivist focus on group interaction and sharing and less on personal independence. It is likely, though, that strong social egalitarian traits within certain Individualist cultures, reflected as low Power-Distance, account for their usage.

When examining resultant behavior on Individualism and Power-Distance, studies of interactions with Wikipedia (Pfeil, Zaphiris, and Ang, 2006) demonstrate the following:

Table 3:   Summary of Correlations of Behavior in Wikipedia (2006) by Cultural Dimension

Behavior	Power-Distance	Individualism
Add Information		-0.98 (p=0.008)
Clarify Information		-0.69 (p=0.155)
Delete Information	-0.72 (p=0.142)	
Delete Link	-0.91 (p=0.047)	
Fix Link		0.84 (p=0.082)
Grammar		0.67 (p=0.163)
Mark-up Language		
Spelling	0.64 (p=0.180)	0.57 (p=0.215)

Pfeil and others (2006) showed a significant negative correlation between the Power-Distance Index and the category Delete Link, as well as a similar trend in Delete Information. It suggests that cultures with a high Power-Distance Index, such as the French, are likely to feel uncomfortable about deleting others' efforts. In a work context, this could suggest that it would be advisable not to expect or require this of people from cultures with high Power-Distance Index in collaborative, online work.

Conclusion

While the world around us is shrinking from a communications vantage point, and the nature versus nurture debate continues, common sense tells us that we are all products of our culture. Culture influences all aspects of our lives, from morals and ethics, to religion, language, and even use of the Internet and the new world of social networking that it brings. These studies show that social networking is not a culturally neutral space, but that differences in behavior across cultures can be observed and measured, giving rise to implications regarding how aspects of collaborative online work are influenced by cultural differences.

Hofstede's work is a reminder that we are still witness to an emerging global culture. Both the differences and similarities between cultures are important to recognize if we are to continue to break down both the virtual and physical barriers between us and learn to connect to one another.

About the Contributing Author

Matthew Hodgson is the Regional-Lead for Web and Information Management with SMS Management & Technology Limited, Canberra, Australia. He has over 10 years experience in e-business strategy, information architecture, information management, and knowledge management underpinned by a comprehensive applied-knowledge of government and international web and information standards, and an intimate understanding of Web 2.0, from folksonomies to wikis and blogs. Matthew has published papers in the areas of social psychology and motivation, and has lectured at the University of Canberra on social computing.

References

Bandura, A. (1977). *Social learning theory.* Englewood Cliffs, NJ: Prentice-Hall.

Basabe, N. and Ros, M. (2005). Cultural dimensions and social behavior correlates: Individualism-Collectivism and Power-Distance. *RIPS/ IRSP,* 18 (1), 189-225 © 2005, Presses Universitaires de Grenoble.

Cummings, J. N., Butler, B., and Kraut, R. (2002). The quality of online social relationships. *Communication of the ACM,* 45 (7), 103-108.

Hofstede, G. (1991). *Cultures and Organizations: Software of the Mind.* London: McGraw-Hill.

Hofstede, G. (2003). *Cultural Dimensions.* Retrieved September 9, 2007, from http://www.geert-hofstede.com/geert_hofstede_resources.shtml

Hofstede, G. J. (2005). *Religion and culture. Correspondence with David Scott.* Retrieved September 8, 2007, from http://www.info.wau.nl/people/gertjan/religion_and_culture.htm

Hui, C. H. and Triandis, H. C. (1986). Individualism-Collectivism. A Study of Cross-Cultural Researchers. *Journal of Cross-Cultural Psychology,* 17(2), 225-248.

Internet Usage Statistics. Retrieved September 8, 2007, from http://www.internetworldstats.com/stats.htm

IPSOS Insight (2007). Image Used with Permission. http://www.ipsosinsight.com/pressrelease.aspx?id=3556

Kemp, M. B., Jaap Favier, J., Josh Bernoff, J., Bouquet, M., and Klevchuk, O. (2007). *Europeans Have Adopted Social Computing Differently.* Retrieved September 9, 2007, from: http://www.forrester.com/ER/Press/Release/0,1769,1154,00.html

Kragh, S. U. and Sven Bislev, B. (2004). *Universities and student values across nations.* Working Paper. Retrieved January 26, 2008 from http://ep.lib.cbs.dk/paper/ISBN/x65644415x

Marcus, A. and Gould, E. W. (2000). Crosscurrents: Cultural dimensions and global web user-interface design. *Interactions*, 7(4), 32-46.

Oyserman, D., Coon, H. M., and Kemmelmeier, M. (2002). Rethinking Individualism and Collectivism: Evaluation of Theoretical assumptions and meta-analyses. *Psychological Bulletin*, 128, 3-72.

Pfeil, U., Zaphiris, P., and Ang, C. S. (2006). Cultural differences in collaborative authoring of Wikipedia. *Journal of Computer-Mediated Communication*, 12(1), 5. Retrieved September 9, 2007 from http://jcmc.indiana.edu/vol12/issue1/pfeil.html

Robbins, S. S. and Stylianou, A. C. (2002). A study of cultural differences in global corporate websites. *Journal of Computer Information Systems*, 42, 3-9.

Schwartz, S. H. (1994). Beyond individualism/collectivism: New cultural dimensions of values. In U. Kim, H.C. Triandis, C. Kagitcibasi, S. Choi, S., and G. Yoon, (Eds.), *Individualism and collectivism: Theory, method and applications* (pp. 85-119). Thousand Oaks, CA: Sage.

Sifry, D. (2006). *State of the Blogosphere, Part 2: On Language and Tagging*. Retrieved September 8, 2007, from http://www.sifry.com/alerts/archives/000433.html

Taylor, J. W., Zhu, G., Dekkers, J., and Marshall, S. (2003). Where Parallels Intersect. *Informing Science InSITE*, June 2003, (pp. 573-587).

Technorati. Retrieved September 8, 2007, from http://technorati.com

Tsikriktsis, N. (2002). Does culture influence web site quality expectations? *Journal of Service Research*, 5 (2), 101-112.

United Nations (2005). United Nations Conference on Trade and Development. UNCTAD Handbook of Statistics.

Wilson, P., Nolla, A., Gunawardena, C., López-Islas, J., Ramírez-Angel, N., and Megchun-Alpírez, R. (2002). A qualitative analysis of online group processes in two cultural contexts. In F. Sudweeks and C. Ess (Eds.), *Proceedings of the Third International Conference on Cultural Attitudes towards Technology and Communication* (pp. 51-68). School of Information Technology: Murdoch University, Australia.

Chapter 9: The Cultural Factors

10 The Influence Factors

Scott Allen

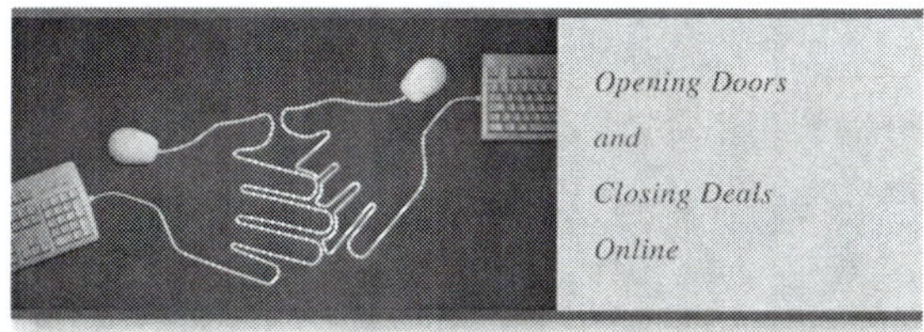

DAVID TETEN and SCOTT ALLEN

Everett Rogers' *Diffusion of Innovations* (2003) is a standard text in the social sciences for looking at how innovations—new technologies—are adopted (or rejected) within social groups. We believe that it complements and serves as a significant reference point for many popular books on the marketing of innovative products, including Geoffrey Moore's *Crossing the Chasm* and Malcolm Gladwell's *The Tipping Point*.

In the book, Rogers (2003) discusses five "perceived characteristics of innovations"—things considered by individuals that affect their potential to move from awareness to adoption:

- **Relative advantage** is the degree to which an innovation is perceived as being better than the idea it supersedes.

- **Compatibility** is the degree to which an innovation is perceived to be consistent with the existing values, past experiences, and needs of potential adopters.

- **Complexity** is the degree to which an innovation is perceived as difficult to use [We will reverse this and refer to "simplicity," so that a higher score in all five areas means more likely adoption].

- **Trialability** is the opportunity to experiment with the innovation on a limited basis.

- **Observability** is the degree to which the results of an innovation are visible to others.

Relative Advantage

In The Relationship Economy, we must realize that social networking sites are not just competing against each other but also against anything and everything vying for the consumer's attention: television, movies, general Web surfing, time with family and friends, work, etc. Social networking sites must offer a relative advantage compared to anything else the consumer could be doing with his or her time.

Among younger users, social networking actually tops the list. In a 2007 study commissioned by MySpace, when asked the question, "If you had 15 minutes of time, which activity would you most like to do?" social networking users age 14-29 said:

17% – Check out social networking sites

17% – Talk on the cell phone

14% – Watch TV

10% – Surf the Web generally

9% – Play video game

8% – Instant Message

7% – Listen to an MP3 player

1% – Listen to the radio

Note: These data do not total 100%. It is possible that the remainder reported as "no preference."

(Never Ending Friending Research Summary, 2007)

Business Networks and Business Applications

Adult users typically have additional needs beyond socialization, including finding a job, making money, and accomplishing business and personal tasks.

A business has presence in a network through its people. A *business network* is a group of people that have some type of commercial relationship, for example, the relationships between boss-employee, buyer-supplier, and colleague-colleague. Business networks leverage firms' offerings and advance their reach to prospective buyers.

Another purpose for a business network is to expand knowledge without extending the users' time. By utilizing the experiences and knowledge of others within their business network, users can work more efficiently in their areas of expertise. As business becomes increasingly globalized, there is a strong need for business networking to take place on a virtual level. There are a myriad of social networking tools that have been created to fulfill these needs. Together with software, which provides access to on-line meetings and instant messaging, people are able to both access and increase their networks of business professionals without traveling.

The advantage of social media in corporations is an undeniable evolution in our corporate world. Well-connected people and well-networked companies are more successful. Organizations with deeper alliances and partnerships lead over the ones that work on their own. However, as the design and current profiles within today's social networks evolve to be more business friendly, we will see mass adoption of social media by businesses.

One of the pre-eminent social networking sites, LinkedIn, is one of the most used business networks precisely because of its focus on productivity. There are no tools for socializing just for the sake of socializing. It is not an open dialog that permits debate, but it allows questions, answers, and clarifications of the question by the original poster. Introduction requests are required to state a specific business purpose including:

- Career opportunities
- Expertise requests
- Consulting offers
- Business deals
- New ventures
- Personal reference requests
- Job inquiries
- Requests to reconnect

Another growing social networking site, Facebook, is also seeing expansion in the area of business applications, and a look at the most popular confirms that meeting basic physiological and safety needs, i.e., finding jobs and earning money, are primary foci.

One of the newest applications is Business 3.0.

     Chapter 10: The Influence Factors

Business 3.0 was launched on Facebook in order to provide business with a presence. Facebook is the first of the social networking sites to offer Business 3.0 and others are in various stages of implementation. Each business that registers on Business 3.0 will have its own business profile, which will include a listing of its products and services, links to business representatives, and e-commerce engines for people to exchange products and services. The rules for business profiling will be different from those for individual profiles. The rules of the game have changed yet again.

Business 3.0 has two major roles. First, it allows businesses to have profiles. Secondly, in the case of Facebook, users can search for a particular business or products from the Business 3.0 application. Adding this application, Facebook users have the ability to search quickly to the business profile they are seeking.

Social networks are quickly becoming ripe ground for businesses to directly market and sell their products and services to people and other businesses. While many may say that is already true today, the difference is that businesses are able to have a direct vs. indirect presence within networks. Business 3.0 will enable businesses to connect with other businesses.

Enabling businesses to have and manage their own profiles within networks and to exchange goods and services may be the process that further ignites the media to be more than a "social network." Many businesses spend thousands of dollars to attend and have a presence at trade shows and conventions throughout any given year. Social networks allow a virtual 24/7 trade show at a fraction of the cost.

Business 3.0 represents an application with magnitude. A small developer is moving faster than the larger ones and continues to develop innovative products. It represents just another "link" in place to usher in The Relationship Economy.

Virtual and Face-to-face Interactions

In addition to beginning to address the needs of businesses through either applications or other features, social networking services compete even more directly with face-to-face networking for participants' attention. If people allocate a relatively fixed amount of time for networking, they have to choose to spend it online or face-to-face, and many still prefer face-to-face because they believe it builds stronger relationships.

However, Teten and Allen (2005) argue in *The Virtual Handshake* that virtual interaction is not inherently inferior, it is just different, and that virtual interaction offers certain advantages over face-to-face:

- Higher Character: You are more likely to be honest, thoughtful, and reflective in your communications in a way that is difficult face-to-face. You can avoid the impulsive emotional responses that often happen face-to-face. You are less likely to be put on the spot in a virtual communication. At the same time, people sometimes will attack one another online in a way they would not do in person.

- Competency: You appear more competent because you can carefully design your responses to accommodate another person's interests. You can simultaneously instant message your colleagues, look up facts in an online encyclopedia or search engine, and use other online resources to increase the appearance of competence. You cannot easily access all those useful resources when talking with people face-to-face (although even that is changing, thanks to the growth of mobile Internet access).

- You can focus your interactions on higher-relevance people. In a face-to-face event, you may spend hours talking with people who are of questionable relevance to your goals. Online, the transition costs are lower; you can simply move on to the most immediately relevant people.

- Simply because you are meeting virtually, you may be able to move more rapidly to a high-strength relationship. You know a great deal about the other person, therefore you have less of a need to spend time on small talk. You also likely selected each other based on common interests and a good business fit. On the other hand, Robert Putnam, author and political scientist, argues that, "the richer the medium of communication, the more sociable, personal, trusting, and friendly the encounter" (Putnam, 2000, p. 176).

    Chapter 10: The Influence Factors

- You can provide better information to people. Because much of the communication is happening in writing, all parties are forced to be clear, and they tend to be more frank.

- You can manage a larger number of relationships by maintaining a basic level of communication with many people. You can communicate simultaneously with thousands of people without having to be a skilled public speaker.

- Even if you sometimes feel awkward meeting people who are different from you, virtual communications allow you to build a far more diverse network. This is particularly true because you may not even be aware of the physical traits of people you meet virtually. However, online networks may be more homogeneous than face-to-face networks in their participants' interests and values.

Opportunities

Services will have to offer functionality or content that helps people accomplish specific objectives in order to stand out from a swarm of MySpace clones. Simply being niche is not enough on its own. Some promising areas for business functionality that are enhanced by integration with social media include:

- Web conferencing
- Calendars
- Event management
- Project management
- Job search/recruiting
- Contact management
- Integrated marketing such as email campaigns, newsletters, etc.
- Document collaboration
- Private virtual workspaces
- Open innovation
- Finding investors or loans
- Making money

Ideas in the consumer space include:

- Weight loss/fitness
- Life goals
- Household/ personal inventory management
- Calendars
- Personal development/self-improvement
- Pet care

Please note the emphasis on functionality *or* content. A site does not necessarily have to provide new technological functionality in order to attract and engage people if it has content that is focused on helping people accomplish goals. For example, a facilitated discussion forum focused on business planning could perhaps be even more effective than simply offering a business plan tool within a site for entrepreneurs.

The key is to focus not just on delivering information or an application, but helping users put it to good business use. Another largely untapped opportunity is for sites to offer free training on how to use their service to accomplish specific tasks. Consider, for example, how Home Depot offers free home improvement workshops. Modifying and applying this model in the social networking space may significantly improve both initial adoption rates and engagement/retention rates.

One of the most important recent developments in this area is the growth of revenue sharing models. Seeing the financial success of ad-supported sites like MySpace and YouTube, many of the users who produce the content and generate the activity that fuels those revenue models are wondering where their share of revenue is, and a growing number of sites are stepping up to the plate to offer it to them. Some of the revenue sharing models currently tested in the marketplace are:

- Direct compensation to content producers for traffic to the content they create (Revver, Helium)

- Enabling users to receive advertising revenue directly (Flixya, HubPages)

- Ecommerce enablement for sharing premium media (FreeIQ)

                    Chapter 10: The Influence Factors

- Network marketing, sharing a portion of premium services with the member's upline (DirectMatches, Friends Win)

- Stock sharing (Ojeez)

- Points and rewards system for blended participation (Gather)

Larger businesses currently using the most popular sites purely for marketing purposes will have no compelling reason to switch to revenue-sharing services, as they are making their money from back-end sales. However, consumers sharing content "just for fun" and even small business owners producing content will be the early adopters of revenue sharing services.

Compatibility

Compatibility is a measure of how well the innovation fits within the existing belief systems and values of potential adopters. This manifests itself in the context of virtual networking in a couple of different ways.

As stated above, one of the most oft-cited objections to virtual networking is that many people believe that "real," i.e., strong, relationships require face-to-face interaction. In spite of seeing the relative advantages, many users are still resistant.

A more complex issue surfaces when a site's functionality does not match with users' expectations of proper social etiquette or functionality. Let us consider some examples:

- The mass migration from Friendster to MySpace was triggered by a combination of these two issues. Friendster did not give users the capability to personalize their profile—a capability readily available with personal Web pages. Friendster also did not offer any kind of group functionality, and when users began creating fake profiles as a primitive sort of group functionality, Friendster shut them down.

- Ryze and LinkedIn both received a mixed reaction when they introduced functionality showing users who had visited their profile. Some users felt it was more like the physical world, in which you could see people walking by, while others felt it was a violation of the paradigm of anonymous web surfing (e.g., while Amazon may know what customers viewed a particular book, the author and publisher of the book do not have access to that information).

- The necessity to reinvite your contacts into each new service you join caused somewhat of a backlash among those people who only wanted to join one or two sites. This gave rise to the term "snam," short for "social networking spam," to refer to the unwanted high volume of invitations from numerous people to join numerous sites (imagine having even 150 friends wanting to connect with you on 10 sites).

- Several sites, including Zero Degrees (now defunct), Doostang, and most recently Quechup, have gone overboard with their efforts to automate the process of inviting people, making it basically a one-click process to invite your entire email address book. The problem is that most people's address books include many people who are not necessarily close friends—they may be someone with whom you had a one-time correspondence, a former employer with whom you are not on good terms, or even a distribution list such as a Yahoo! Group (the largest LinkedIn-related Yahoo! Group frequently receives invitation connections to various sites).

The issue in each of these cases is that the functionality of the site differed substantially from the user's expectations based on either social behavioral norms or other Web applications.

Opportunities

People's beliefs and value systems typically do not change quickly. The most effective means for overcoming resistance in these areas is education on the relative advantages, particularly in ways that subtly demonstrate errors in the existing beliefs. For example, educating members on the advantages of virtual interaction could help overcome resistance from people who have a very strong preference for face-to-face interaction.

Ensuring that functionality offered by the site is as consistent as possible with traditional social behavior norms is very important. For example:

- Many users view pre-written "canned" invitations provided by the site as impersonal and dehumanizing. Allowing, or even forcing, users to create their own personal invitation message might require a little more effort on their part, but it makes the whole process much more compatible with existing social behavior paradigms.

- Users should have a high degree of control over what personal information is displayed to whom, who can contact them and for what purposes, their visibility when browsing others' profiles, etc.

We recommend reviewing major new functionality in this context before implementation.

Simplicity & Trialability

Most social networking sites are relatively simple to try—fill out a basic registration form, confirm your email address, and you are accepted. The potential downside of an easy registration process, though, is that effective engagement in a virtual social network typically requires more than simply group interaction—it requires the creation of a user profile and establishing connections, mostly with people the user already knows who are also members.

When viewed from the perspective of a single site, the trialability issue seems trivial, but when considering that a user may be a member of a dozen or more sites, and that this will only continue to grow as social software becomes integral to commerce sites, it becomes a major issue. This is particularly true for sites in which participation will be light to moderate, such as brand-sponsored communities, as users will be judging whether the relative value of participation exceeds the time cost of becoming fully engaged in the site.

Another issue regarding trialability concerns sites whose business model includes premium services. Is there a free membership level? Does it provide sufficient functionality for users to make an informed decision about upgrading to the premium service level? Is there a free trial period, and if so, what happens at the end of the free trial?

Opportunities

The primary challenge is to make the establishment of user identity and relationship data as simple as possible, in order that users can start realizing the full benefits of membership as soon as possible.

Currently, the most common solution is to provide the ability to import contacts from an email address book, identify those that are also members of the service, and send them a connection request. Some sites also allow members to invite contacts from their address book to the service. While this does simplify the process, as described earlier, making it too simple presents its own set of problems.

One important factor to consider when targeting business users is that many businesses do not use Web-based mail systems such as GMail, AOL, Yahoo! Mail or Hotmail as their business email system. Functionality should be included to import contacts from Outlook or an export from a contact management or CRM system. An even better solution is to provide a direct integration into these systems, as LinkedIn has done with their Outlook plug-in.

There are better solutions currently available that are increasing in popularity. New services entering the marketplace or those looking to increase membership should consider using one of the technologies, such as federated identity management, that simplifies the process of creating a profile. Developing technologies in portability of social network data will further improve this area.

Regarding premium services, both the "freemium" model (free basic service with a premium service offered on a subscription basis) and the free trial model, as well as models blending the two, have proven effective. The biggest concern in both cases is the "ghost town effect" that occurs when the free membership is so highly restricted as to cause users to stop participation.

For example, Classmates.com, one of the oldest social networking sites, boasts 50 million registered user accounts but only 2.7 million paid accounts. Their recent S-1 filing for their pending IPO offers insight into the problem:

> We may not be successful in increasing or maintaining the number of paying subscribers for our social networking services. Only a small percentage of members initially registering for our social networking services sign up for a paid subscription at the time of registration. As a result, our ability to generate subscription revenue is highly dependent on our ability to convince free members to return to our Web sites and become paying subscribers. The number of free members returning to our Web sites has been decreasing, and if we were to continue to experience such decreases, it would likely adversely impact our number of paying subscribers.
>
> Although we have recently experienced an increase in the number of paying subscribers, this trend may not continue. Most of our paying subscribers elect to purchase our services as a result of a limited number of features. For example, we believe that our recently introduced Classmates digital guestbook feature is responsible for a significant portion of the increase in our new pay accounts since the end of 2006. If our social networking pay features are not as compelling and we do not stay current with evolving consumer trends, our free members may not subscribe for our pay features. Any decrease in our conversion rate of free members into paying subscribers could adversely affect our business and financial results.
>
> Since the beginning of 2006, an average of four to six percent of our paying subscribers each month decides not to renew their subscriptions, which we refer to as "churn." The level of churn we experience fluctuates from quarter to quarter due to a variety of factors, including our mix of subscription terms, which affects the timing of subscription expirations. We must continually add new subscribers both to replace subscribers who elect not to renew their subscriptions and to grow our business beyond our current subscriber base. (SEC, 2007)

Many users have criticized Classmates' highly restrictive free functionality, which allows members to establish profiles, search for other members, and read public message boards; posting messages or contacting other members requires a premium membership. Other sites with similar models, such as Ecademy, have garnered similar criticism. While there is nothing inherently wrong with this business model, it may generate more customer ill will than those with less restrictive free membership functionality.

We recommend that unless compelling ROI can be demonstrated in other ways, companies offer a free level of basic membership that has sufficient functionality to keep people engaged on an ongoing basis. This not only creates customer goodwill, but also generally offers increased value to premium members by having a larger pool of engaged users available for search and interaction.

Observability

Clearly, a user knows if he or she has received a tangible benefit such as finding a job or making a sale because of his or her participation. However, until a major transaction results, how can they see progress because of their activities? Moreover, how do users learn about the successes of others who are using the system?

LinkedIn provides a visual metric that allows users to measure their progress:

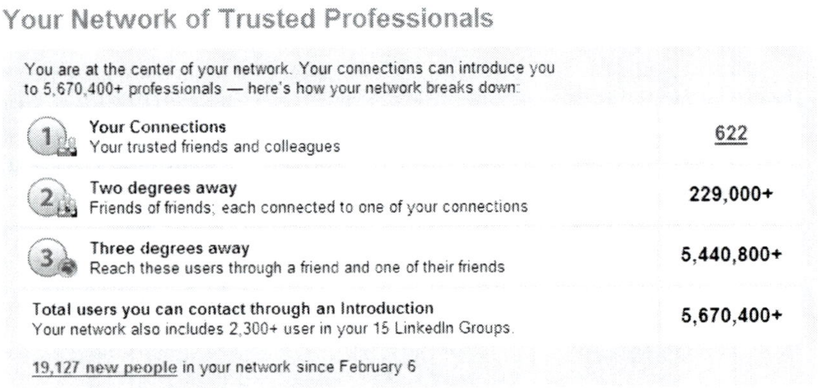

Figure 7: Screen Shot from LinkedIn

                    Chapter 10: The Influence Factors

Endorsements and recommendations offer another publicly visible sign that the person's social networking activity is "doing something" by helping them build their reputation.

Opportunities

Revenue sharing, as described earlier, is a concrete way to provide observable benefits from active participation. Offer incentives for people to engage in the behavior that you want them to engage in either on an ongoing basis or as a single campaign. For example, a campaign by Gather offered $20 Borders gift certificates for successfully inviting five new people to join.

Another underutilized opportunity is to show aggregate performance metrics. These help give hope to users who have not experienced concrete results. For example, InnerSell and Ecademy both prominently feature testimonials on their home page such as:

- "Thanks to InnerSell I have a new $50,000 customer."

- "I closed a deal with first year revenues of $50,000 within a week of getting the InnerSell lead."

- "InnerSell has boosted my business by 25%."

- "I have made directly or indirectly over £10,000 through Ecademy since I joined."

Most sites do not have this, and we have been unable to locate one reporting any kind of aggregate success metrics.

Contrast this with, for example, eHarmony. On its main site navigation, there is a link to a page featuring dozens of success stories, and their "Why eHarmony" page, also linked in the main navigation, proudly proclaims, "90 eHarmony members get married every single day."

Sites can significantly differentiate themselves by tracking and publicly reporting user success metrics as well as anecdotal success stories.

Conclusion

Many new sites use a "bells and whistles" approach or target a specific niche in order to find a substantial user base. We believe, though, that in this increasingly competitive marketplace, understanding the complex and often unspoken needs of users is essential—not only in the messaging used to attract users but also in site design and content planning—in order to keep users engaged and encourage word-of-mouth marketing to grow membership. Revenue sharing and the collection and publication of performance metrics are two of the most important opportunities for companies to differentiate themselves.

References

Never Ending Friending Research Summary. (2007, April 12). Retrieved December 5, 2007 from http://ibiblio.org/fred/stuff/40161_NEF.pdf

Putnam, R. (2000). *Bowling Alone*. New York: Touchstone Books.

Rogers, E. (2003). *Diffusion of Innovations* (5th ed.). New York: Free Press.

SEC – Securities & Exchange Commission (2007). Classmates Media Corporation, Form S-1 Registration Statement, filed August 13, 2007: www.sec.gov/Archives/edgar/data/1409112/000104746907006388/a2179103zs-1.htm http://tinyurl.com/2tzkdy

Teten, D. and Allen, S. (2005). *The Virtual Handshake: Opening Doors and Closing Deals Online*. New York: AMACOM, 2005. Available at http://thevirtualhandshake.com

The Media Factors

Jay T. Deragon

The Relationship Economy is causing a shift in thinking of not only the value of relationships, but also in determining the significance of the multitude of networks that are increasing in strength and intensity every single day of the year.

eMarketer, a Market Research on E-Business and Online Marketing service, estimates that in 2007, companies will spend more than $1 billion worldwide—on social network advertising alone. Although the lead players, MySpace and Facebook, are expected to continue their strong performance, hundreds of new social networking sites will give them competition. No longer can smaller, decentralized networks be dismissed as fads that will simply initially flourish and then subsequently fizzle (eMarketer, 2007).

"The Social Network Marketing Report" analyzes the trends that are driving new competitors into one of the hottest advertising spaces on the Internet. Since eMarketer published its first report on social network marketing, companies have latched on with almost religious fervor onto the notion that consumers want to be socially connected on-line—whether on mass-appeal sites such as MySpace, on targeted niche sites and video sites, or on mobile phones—almost everywhere.

However, is there enough interest among consumers in social networking to support so many ventures? Reports suggest this is indeed the case.

Even analysts do not recognize that soon much of this ad revenue will be going to individuals who emerge as the market makers by leveraging their own personal networking portals for products and services to others and by being a natural advertising venue for related brands.

Your best hope is scattering your portion of content ubiquitously throughout the Web and on all new devices to use Netizens' paths to grab brief attention. For marketers, it is a direct-response medium.

Companies whose traditional approach is massive brand-building advertising are on-line, pitted against companies whose *only* advertising is a direct sales pitch. Internet media to date has best served the direct-response world, with 80 percent of dollar spending. There is no way to measure next month's return, let alone next quarter's or next year's return, by the actions marketers take today on the Web. Moreover, brand marketers, in the absence of proof, have largely just stayed away (ironic, because they spend billions off-line, sometimes with little proof of effectiveness).

As brand-marketing looks poised to ramp up intensity, tensions are growing between the needs of brand-advertising and direct-response advertising, and all marketers are seeking new ways to use the Internet that can transcend the traditional brand versus direct-response calculus. How do you organize to engage in the individual conversations promised by the medium and demanded by the consumer? How does a marketer operate within an environment that is simultaneously global and hyper-targeted, while the relentless drumbeat for improved returns on investments keeps average chief marketing officers' tenures to less than 24 months?

The answer to this shifting audience relationship is for advertisers and marketers to focus on you: **YOUR** brand, not theirs.

The Relationship Economy will usher in a new era of mediums for advertisers seeking to match their product/service with an affinity of your brand's preferences and privileges. As individuals further the creation of their brands, on numerous social networks, their connections and conversations provide specific data that identifies an audience with specific affinities to specific branded products and services—an advertiser's dream of target marketing.

Market research firm, Compete, Inc., (2007) released a report on the convergence of social networking and e-commerce. The report, "s-commerce: beyond MySpace and YouTube," finds consumer visits to social networking sites have increased 109 percent since January 2004, and page views per visitor have grown by 414 percent in the same time period. Social networkers, according to the report, spend less time viewing traditional media. Those same social networkers have more discretionary income and a greater penchant for online shopping than non-social networking site users (Nelson, 2006).

"Some marketers are going to advertise on MySpace and YouTube because they are the two easiest places to go. That will be an obvious choice. But the return on investment isn't going to be any better than traditional customer acquisition campaigns," said Ross Dawson (2007), strategy consultant, bestselling author, and CEO of consulting firm Advanced Human Technologies. "It's stupid to just advertise on MySpace and assume you are a social marketer. The better thing to do is get your customers associated with your brand," Dawson said. (Dawson, 2007)

On the other hand, launching a *branded* social network means competing for a dwindling slice of end users' attention. Compete, Inc. (2007) found visitors to social networking services are currently involved with an average of three such sites, and would only be willing to add a fourth Web site before losing interest.

Stephen DiMarco, Vice President and Chief Marketing Officer of Compete, Inc., warns others about the future of marketing on social networks: "Already people are starting to become social-saturated. For marketers, there are not going to be as many opportunities as they think there are. So they need to be more creative" (Compete, 2007). The key is to create social Web sites as part of a brand, designed to track customers and listen to them at the same time.

When you have your own personal network portal, you will control your own network of connections, articles, news, videos, documents, and related media. As an individual with certain affinities, shown by the data in your network, you will be able to indicate what your network (think: contacts) is inclined to purchase at any given time. The value to advertisers is by forming a relationship with you and your network with your permission, and is directly proportional to one's affinities, reach, value, propositions, connections, and profile. If your network creates traffic and establishes connections to like-minded individuals and businesses, then your network is a distribution point of reach.

Table 4:   U.S. Weekly Radio Audience Estimated for 2007 (eMarketer, 2007)

U.S. Weekly Radio Audience Estimated for 2007 *(millions of listeners)*	
Terrestrial radio	282.8
Internet radio	29.0
Podcasting	7.1
Mobile phone audio streaming	4.1
High-definition radio	0.5
Source: eMarketer, 2007, from Bridge Ratings, Arbitron, Edison	

In The Relationship Economy, your brand creates commerce through sharing value. Your brand generates revenue, and if someone wants to advertise on the back of your brand, he or she will pay based on your metrics, your value, your reach, and the richness of your relationships.

This new paradigm in advertising models will require advertising executives to rethink their entire approach to The Relationship Economy. They will realize that the best thing for them to do is to get their brand associated with *your* brand. Then and only then will marketers achieve success in reaching the masses, or the grassroots targets: consumers.

Online Ads Trump Radio in 2008

Ben Macklin, Senior Analyst of the company eMarketer and author of the report "Radio Trends," says that advertising revenues on Internet radio, satellite radio, podcasting, high-definition radio and mobile devices will surpass spending in traditional radio venues in 2008. The new study concludes, "Traditional radio is rapidly being subsumed into a new, broader sector called 'audio'" (eMarketer, 2007).

Table 5:   Media Use Per Day by U.S. Adult Internet Users (eMarketer, 2007)

Media Use Per Day by U.S. Adult Internet Users (January, 2007)				
Media	Echo Boomers (18-31)	GenX (32-42)	Baby Boomers (42-62)	Total Mean Hours/Day
Internet	3.28	3.00	2.69	2.91
TV	2.73	2.63	2.83	2.78
Radio	1.79	1.88	1.93	1.87
Source: eMarketer, April 2007, from Lumin Collaborative				

According to Lumin Collaborative, cited in the study, traditional radio is losing its significance in people's lives. US adults are spending more time each day on the Internet and watching TV than listening to the radio, asserts Macklin. Macklin's conclusion for advertisers is, "There are...many synergies between radio and the Internet, and for the most part they complement rather than compete with each other" (eMarketer, 2007).

Therefore, The Relationship Economy and your brand, along with its network, will most likely have advertisers searching for you and, in particular, the best-connected individuals with the highest developed networks, both in quantity and quality, rather than searching for big companies and large advertising firms.

References

Compete, Inc. (2007, October 11). *New Research Reveals Next Wave of Social Networking Opportunities: New "s–commerce" strategies seamlessly integrate commercial and social web.* Retrieved October 10, 2007, from http://www.competeinc.com/news_events/pressReleases/168

Dawson, R. (2007, August 17). *Marketers accepting loss of control is on the way to the mainstream.* Retrieved January 20, 2008, from http://www.rossdawsonblog.com/weblog/archives/2007/08

eMarketer (2007). *Internet Radio to Outstrip HD Radio: Internet radio legal squabbles won't stop growth.* Retrieved October 18, 2007, from http://www.emarketer.com/Article.aspx?id=1005243

Nelson, M. G. (2006, October 12). Social Media and E-Commerce Converging: Report, The ClickZ Network, October 12, 2006. Retrieved October 12, 2007, from http://www.clickz.com/3623667

12 The Gender Factors

Carter F. Smith

Gender differences will be with us for eternity and therefore, we need to examine how those differences will affect an individual's participation in The Relationship Economy. Individuals have dealt with gender differences in a variety of ways over the years, but only recently have those differences been examined seriously in the context of professional interaction. In order to establish a framework, we will examine gender differences here in the context of networking, a critical element in the lives of all people as we collectively engage The Relationship Economy.

In the late 1980s, personal social networks were defined as "a collection of individuals who know and interact with a particular target individual or couple" (Defining Social Networks, 2007). In the

1990s, many studies focused on differences in gender as they related to networking and technology (APC, 1996; Ebben and Kramarae, 1993; Hardings and McGregor, 1996; Huyer, 1997; Moser, 1993; Redwood, 1996; Shade, 1993). As we enter The Relationship Economy in 2008, it is important that we focus specifically on networking using technology.

In "The Gender Factors," we examine some of the differences in the ways men and women engage in networking. We will look at how women use technology. We will study networking behavior, and we will attempt to explain the importance of networking—specifically online networking—in The Relationship Economy.

Many of us are experiencing terminology challenges as we explore the online world of social networking. Some use the term "social networking" to identify the action of building one's network, whether in the real or virtual world. Others limit their use of the term to those actions where they are adding and cultivating relationships with friends and acquaintances they have officially connected with on an online social networking site. Others distinguish between the connections made for business and for non-business, personal reasons.

In order to examine gender differences, we have adopted the following definitions:

Networking: The action involved in building one's network of friends and acquaintances, whether for personal or professional reasons (or both).

Online networking: The action involved in building one's network of friends and/or acquaintances, whether for personal or professional reasons, in the online environment.

Differences in How Men and Women Network

When we are involved in group or community activities, do we pay attention to how different people participate in or contribute to the group dynamic? Are there tangible differences based on more than just personality or position? In the traditional family, the gender roles were often easily identified, but how about group interaction in The Relationship Economy—are there differences that we need to consider? Forret and

Dougherty (2001) recently observed that demographic characteristics including gender, along with personality and attitudinal characteristics were related to our involvement in networking behavior.

Gilligan (1982) observed that in contemporary society, women were seen (and expected to be seen) through lenses that were designed for seeing men. She noted that this view of women was distorted and could not be reconciled without a complete adjustment in the way women are perceived in society (1982). Her observations were not made in the context of the online environment, but her perceptions were valid—at least for the time. Has society made the necessary adjustment?

Herring (1994) found that men and women participate differently in online discussions. She found that the ethical framework for online communications was different for men than it is for women. Primarily, men were more likely to send angry or insulting messages on discussion boards, while women tended to be more accepting of different views in the online forums (1994).

Herring (1994) observed that men operated with a different value system, under which they assigned greater value to freedom from censorship, open expression, and debate. Women, on the other hand, tended to feel they must be "sensitive to the wishes of all participants for the benefit of the entire community" (Githens, 1996). So how do these drastically different styles ever converge or communicate?

In studies of faculty in higher education before the advent of contemporary social networking technology, Rothstein and Davey (1995) found that women tended to interact more with women and men tended to interact more with men in their interpersonal networks. They found, though, that despite this tendency towards segregated networks, women did not seem disadvantaged (Rothstein and Davey, 1995). This self-segregation appeared to be chosen, rather than directed. Was there an underlying purpose?

Rothstein and Davey (1995) learned that female faculty received more support from their networks than did men, and they realized the importance of social support more, and worked to extend their networks accordingly. Does this mean that women are inherently better networkers, or could it be that they are better able to recognize the need for networking in the first place? Unlike the findings in the education sector, in many business organizations, women were segregated from men's networks and found it more difficult to obtain the benefits that those networks provided (Rothstein and Davey, 1995).

Githens (1996) noted that "Computer-Mediated Communication" (CMC), which is similar to today's online communications environment, provided an environmental extension of the ways in which human beings already communicated. She noted that this environment was often liberating, and duplicated all the misunderstandings and confusion that took place in the interactions between men and women in everyday life (1996).

Some of the "differences in communications" seen by Herring (1994), when combined with Githens' (1996) "misunderstandings and confusion" are troublesome when considered in the context of online communications.

The subjective nature of appraisal and promotion systems has long been seen as a barrier for women, especially where gender stereotyping persists (Singh, Kumra, and Vinnicombe, 2002). Because women naturally tend to underrate their achievements and often have less confidence in their abilities than their managers have for them, women who are assertive and confident are more likely to be evaluated negatively (Singh et al., 2002). So how do these challenges affect networking?

Both men and women viewed networking as important for career advancement (Singh et al., 2002). Men often see networking as a key and necessary activity—a method with which to enhance their personal and professional reputation; women see networking as central to developing a professional profile and building a reputation as someone who is competent and capable of delivering (2002). These two views may initially seem similar, except that the men did not address the same concerns for demonstrating competence within their network. There was some concern expressed that networking was not a natural activity for women (2002).

Could it be that we are living out the traditional roles that we feel were assigned to us at birth? It is known that girls play most often in twos, while boys often play in groups or teams (Singh et al., 2002). The traditional feminine role encourages the display of emotional dependence on others, while the male role encourages strength and individuality (2002).

Men may be more motivated to use their networking to achieve career goals (Hetty van Emmerik, Euwema, Geschiere, and Schouten, 2006). Would that explain the differences we see in networking strategy? Hetty van Emmerik et al. (2006) examined gender differences in both formal and informal network participation and found that it was positively associated with career satisfaction, and found that career satisfaction appeared stronger for men than for women. (Hetty van Emmerik et al., 2006). Does this mean that women would be more satisfied with their careers if they did more networking? Surely, there is a place for both roles in The Relationship Economy.

Women and Technology

A decade ago, Advancing Women Inc. (AWI) reported that it was critical for women to be connected to the Internet in order to access the available news, research, and information, as well as to have the opportunity to debate, communicate, and engage in the intellectual growth and stimulation—all of which interaction with new technology brings (AWI, 1998). Note that the ability to successfully network online depends (as before) on *access* (Srinivas, 2007).

Perhaps part of the problem is that women are often seen as simply consumers of information and services—not as providers or generators (Srinivas, 2007). What would cause this perception to change? Much of the recent developments in the realm of networking are technology-based. As such, it is essential that sufficient access to technology is available in traditional education.

Smith's (2005) study found no differences between men and women regarding access to technology courses, but identified notable differences in the number of such courses taken by women. This suggested that the education system's ability to provide access to computer and information technology courses may (ultimately) serve to bridge the gap between men and women in this area, but we are still left wondering how (or if) to close the gap sooner.

Perhaps if more women were involved in the technology sector, a shift would naturally occur. It appears that women may avoid technology positions based on deeply entrenched negative stereotypes. Although females possess the ability to learn and use computers, they often do not want to be associated with the "geeky" image of technical careers (Gilbert, Lee-Kelley and Barton, 2003). Some women may feel unable to fight the overriding stereotype that those who work in technology are nerds or geeks with a boring job (Lee, 2005). Jobs in the technology sector may be considered male-oriented, especially those with more "macho" titles, like "computer engineer." Lee (2005) observed that these mental images form between the ages of 11 and 13. If presented in a particular way, technology-related work could appeal as much, or more, to young girls, rather than predominantly to boys (Lee, 2005).

One of the more recent areas of growth may provide a glimpse of the natural potential for women to engage in online social networking communities. The expansion of higher education into the online environment has provided many adults with the opportunity to complete (or advance) their level of education. As part of the educational package, many institutions provide (and require participation in) a venue for interacting with others while discussing assorted topics related to the courses attended. This interaction can foster a sense of community, learning, and ultimately retention. The venues are based on not-so-new technology, delivered in the form of an asynchronous discussion area where students respond to course-related questions asked by the professor and then engage others in conversation on related topics.

Rovai and Baker (2005) found that students adopting the connected pattern of socialization in society (usually women) were more likely to seek membership in learning communities than their status-seeking (often male) counterparts. It has been shown that students in traditional learning environments with a strong sense of community are more likely to complete the program than those who do not. Studies in the online classroom have reached similar conclusions (Rovai and Baker, 2005).

The primary intent of Rovai and Baker's (2005) study was to determine whether men and women differed in their sense of classroom community and level of perceived learning. Their study provided a foundation for examining the changes in dynamics that we can expect in the professional world of The Relationship Economy. It also provides insight into the workings of the online social networking world, where many men and women of all ages are already engaged in these types of asynchronous communications and other activities.

The asynchronous online environment is one that appears to be hospitable to women. Women posted significantly more messages in course discussion boards than did men, though men tended to dominate conversations on occasion (Rovai and Baker, 2005). So what would explain the more active participation by the women in this study? Perhaps the discussion-rich online learning environment is particularly well suited to women who have been seen as more responsive to social reinforcement and extrinsic motivation than men (Rovai and Baker, 2005).

Networking Behavior

Although the importance of networking is increasingly well recognized, we still know little about the attributes of those who engage in networking behaviors (Forret and Dougherty, 2001). Forret and Dougherty (2001) found five dimensions of networking behavior resulted from their analysis: maintaining contacts, socializing, engaging in professional activities, participating in church and community, and increasing internal visibility. Both men and women engage in these activities, so that does not appear to explain the differences in application.

Professionals in the early career stages may perceive that networking is an important tool for promoting their careers, though they typically have fewer colleagues and contacts in the industry or profession. As a result, building a network becomes a method to gain assistance as well as recognition (Forret and Dougherty, 2001). In contrast, employees with more work experience, in the later career stages, may feel their careers have plateaued and that networking is a waste of time and effort (Forret and Dougherty, 2001). We need to find a way for those in need of experienced advice to meet with those who have it.

We know a bit about how networking works. Networking includes behaviors that help bring in more business for the organization and fulfill public relations strategies (Forret and Dougherty, 2001). These networking behaviors include taking current and potential clients to dinners and sporting events, accepting speaking engagements, participating in civic affairs, joining industry or professional associations, taking an active role in community projects, and engaging in athletic activities (2001).

Networking behaviors include actions intended to develop and maintain relationships with others who have the potential to assist them in their work or career (Forret and Dougherty, 2001). Networking should be a proactive venture, though—not a reactive response. Strategic networking arrangements rely on cooperative behavior as a means of competing in decidedly aggressive markets and in the face of environmental uncertainty (Miller, Besser and Riibe, 2006).

Two job characteristics were particularly important regarding networking behavior. An individual's organizational level and the type of position he or she holds may influence networking behaviors (Forret and Dougherty, 2001). Initially, this may give some insight to the differences, as women traditionally lack representation at these levels. As one rises in the organizational ranks, expectations increase for developing new client relationships, playing active roles in professional organizations, and taking more visible assignments within the organization (2001). Is the need for networking limited to high-ranking executives who love to be competitive?

In the past, men engaged in networking behavior more frequently than women, but as women become more aware of the importance of networking to their careers, they are beginning to engage in these behaviors to a similar extent as males. Certainly, networking is openly discussed now, as evidenced by numerous articles, books, clubs, and development workshops on the topic (Forret and Dougherty, 2001).

There is good reason to think that networking comes naturally for women. Traits that have traditionally been identified in our culture as feminine (cooperating, building relationships, helping, and developing others) are also those necessary in networking, as opposed to the classical masculine notions of directing and controlling (Forret and Dougherty, 2001). Men were found to be more likely to engage in socializing behaviors than women were, though this increased socializing might have been due to women having less after-hours socializing time because of family responsibilities (Forret and Dougherty, 2001).

The practice of networking has a long and well-developed history. Networking can be viewed as a useful business strategy or action taken to improve the economic status of one's business (Miller, Besser, and Riibe, 2006). In any event, networking happens more often, and is catalyzed by the recent introduction of a variety of Web sites dedicated to its application.

How Important Is It?

We recognize the gender differences, and we see that women are well suited for networking. What can be accomplished with networking in addition to talking to a number of people? Is there actually some value?

The value of new technology increases with the number of adopters. This is closely related to the concept of networking. As more and more individuals in a social network adopt the interactive methods, its use is more beneficial to both previous and potential adopters (Ilie, Van Slyke, Green, and Lou, 2005).

Men and women have different perceptions of communication mediums and media, and those differences in perceptions cause men and women to communicate at different levels, perceive their community differently, and have differing views on a variety of topics (Rovai and Baker, 2005). Real-time communication mediums are capable of providing a feeling of connectedness, as they allow individuals the ability to be part of a group for exchanging information and knowledge (Ilie et al., 2005). This becomes more significant as we progress through The Relationship Economy.

Understanding gender differences for leaders in large organizations is critical. As the number of remote or virtual workers increases across the globe, assumptions are often made about their work habits, behaviors, and perceptions in lieu of the face-to-face observations in a traditional place of business (Ilie et al., 2005). These perceptions may be affected by many of the assumptions and stereotypes addressed here. Understanding how men and women differ in their perceptions would give virtual managers a better feel for how men and women communicate and what they value more (Ilie et al., 2005). This would help them improve communication between geographically separated co-workers, with the result being more effectiveness in their organizations (Ilie et al., 2005).

Gender differences for small business owners in The Relationship Economy are important to consider as well. Traditionally, female-owned businesses have had lower sales volume and earnings than male-owned businesses (Miller, Besser, and Riibe, 2006). Networking may be beneficial in this regard, as it may increase the chances for success for women who desire to start or grow a business.

Networks may be used to obtain strategic advice, creditors, and suppliers, and membership and participation in a business or trade network can provide opportunities for women to make such contacts (Miller, Besser, and Riibe, 2006).

The challenge is to get involved in and find a way to contribute to these professional networks. Getting involved is the critical first step. Women increase their access to expert advice when they move beyond their more traditional social networks of family and friends and seek memberships in business networks (Miller, Besser, and Riibe, 2006).

Though some individuals are more naturally inclined to engage in networking behaviors than others, many learned behaviors can further networking skills and opportunities. The human interaction found in the process of pursuing additional degree or nondegree educational programs can enlarge the network of contacts (Forret and Dougherty, 2001). Individuals may also seek training and assistance in developing their interpersonal skills, or look for a mentor within their organization to help them meet people they should know (Forret and Dougherty, 2001). Ultimately, the important steps are finding common ground with others, and then identifying ways to collaborate for mutual benefit.

Conclusion

As we all progress through The Relationship Economy, there will be many opportunities for success—both personal and professional. For both men and women, success depends on understanding and capitalizing on individual strengths, and supplementing individual strengths with the strengths of those in our networks. Networking helps us leverage the strengths of others and provides an environment that fosters collaboration.

Technological advances within the medium of social networks will evolve, and regardless of gender, the process will enable all to express themselves both as individuals and collectively as groups with common affinities. The collective exchange of ideas will create new value propositions; opportunities will continue to develop; and we will be better prepared to bridge the gap between the genders and enable growth and collaboration beyond measure.

The connectivity afforded by online social networking provides fertile ground for improved relations, new opportunities, and benefits that extend beyond all existing understanding of human interaction and the related dynamics for both genders. These new discoveries will serve to usher in The Relationship Economy, where everyone has the opportunity to win.

References

APC - Association for Progressive Communications (1996). Global Networking for Change: Experiences from the APC Woman's Program. *Survey findings (May 1997) of the APC Women's Networking Survey.* San Francisco: Association for Progressive Communications.

AWI - Advancing Women Inc. (1998). Women's Role in Networking on the Net. International Business & Career Community. Retrieved October 10, 2007, from http://www.advancingwomen.com/webnetwrk5html

Defining Social Networks (2007). *Marriage and Family Encyclopedia.* Retrieved October 10, 2007, from http://family.jrank.org/pages/1601/ Social-Networks-Defining-Social-Networks.html http://tinyurl.com/3aup69

Ebben, M. and Kramarae, C. (1993). Women and Information Technologies: Creating a Cyberspace of our own. In Taylor, Kramarae, and Ebben (eds.) *Women, Information Technology and Scholarship.* Urbana, Ill: WITS Colloqium, Center for Advanced Study.

Forret, M. L. and Dougherty, T. W. (2001). Correlates of networking behavior for managerial and professional employees. *Group & Organization Management,* 26(3), 283-311.

Gilbert, D., Lee-Kelley, L., and Barton, M. (2003). Technophobia, gender influences and consumer decision-making for technology-related products. *European Journal of Innovation Management,* 6(4), 253-263.

Gilligan, C. (1982). *In a Different Voice*. Cambridge, MA: Harvard University Press.

Githens, S. (1996). *Gender Styles in Computer Mediated Communication (CMC)*. Retrieved October 10, 2007, from http://www9.georgetown.edu/faculty/bassr/githens/covr511.htm

Hardings, S. and McGregor, E. (1996). The Gender Dimension of Science and Technology. *World Science Report*. Paris: UNESCO.

Herring, S. (1994). *Gender Differences in Computer-Mediated Communication: Bringing Familiar Baggage to the New Frontier.* Retrieved October 10, 2007, from http://w2.eff.org/Net_culture/Gender_issues/cmc_and_gender.article

Hetty van Emmerik, I.J., Euwema, M. C., Geschiere, M., and Schouten, M. (2006). Networking your way through the organization: Gender differences in the relationship between network participation and career satisfaction. *Women in Management Review,* 21(1), 54-66.

Huyer, S. (1997), Supporting women's use of information technologies for sustainable development. *Report submitted to the Gender and Sustainable development Unit, IDRC*. Ottawa: International Development Research Center.

Ilie, V., Van Slyke, C., Green, G., and Lou, H. (2005). Gender Differences in Perceptions and Use of Communication Technologies: A Diffusion of Innovation Approach. *Information Resources Management Journal,* 18(3), 13-31.

Lee, L. (2005). Tackling Technology's Image Problem Among Young Girls. *The International Journal of Sociology and Social Policy,* 25(10/11), 119-130.

Miller, N. J., Besser, T. L., and Riibe, J. V. (2006). Do Strategic business networks benefit male- and female-owned small-community businesses? *Journal of Small Business Strategy,* 17(2), 53-74.

Moser, O.N.C. (1993). *Gender Planning and Development: Theory, Practice and Training*. London: Routledge.

Redwood, R. (1996). Channels for Change, *Keynote address for WITI's Channels for Change 1996 Conference.* Women in Technology International (WITI).

Rothstein, M. G. and Davey, L. M. (1995). Gender differences in network relationships in academia. *Women in Management Review,* 10(6), 20.

Rovai, A. P. and Baker, J. D. (2005). Gender differences in online learning: Sense of community, perceived learning, and interpersonal interactions. *Quarterly Review of Distance Education,* 6(1), 31-44,85-86.

Shade, L. (1993, August 17-19). Gender Issues in Computer Networking. *Text of talk given at Community Networking: The International Free-Net Conference.* Ottawa, Canada.

Singh, V., Kumra, S., and Vinnicombe, S. (2002). Gender and impression management: Playing the promotion game. *Journal of Business Ethics,* 2, 37(1), 77.

Smith, S. M. (2005). The digital divide: Gender and racial differences in information technology education. *Information Technology, Learning, and Performance Journal,* 23(1), 13-23.

Srinivas, H. (2007). *Online Technology and Networking: Some Gender Perspectives.* Retrieved October 30, 2007, from http://www.gdrc.org/gender/ait-paper.html

13 The Age Factors

Scott Allen

Early adoption of social media and social networking has been most prominent in the 14-24 age group, but accelerated significantly in 2006-2007 in older age groups. As is expected, business-oriented sites such as LinkedIn, Xing, Ryze, and Ecademy have a much older demographic than sites used more for social purposes. The largest sites, MySpace and Facebook, are the sites experiencing the most significant upward age shift. Younger users are also far more likely to use instant messaging, blogs, virtual worlds, and online games as an alternative to widely used forms of communication, such as email.

An August 2006 analysis from comScore Media Matrix demonstrates the disproportionate rate of adoption among younger users on the leading social networking sites:

Table 6:   Demographic Profile of Visitors to Select Social Networking Sites (Lipsman, 2006a)

Demographic Profile of Visitors to Select Social Networking Sites
Percent Composition of Total Unique Visitors, August 2006
Total U.S. – Home/Work/University Locations
Source: comScore Media Metrix

| | Percent (%) Composition of Unique Visitors | | | | |
	Total Internet	MySpace	Facebook	Friendster	Xanga
Unique Visitors (000)	*173,407*	*55,778*	*14,782*	*1,043*	*8,066*
Total Audience	100.0	100.0	100.0	100.0	100.0
Persons: 12-17	9.6	11.9	14.0	10.6	20.3
Persons: 18-24	11.3	18.1	34.0	15.6	15.5
Persons: 25-34	14.5	16.7	8.6	28.2	11.0
Persons: 35-54	38.5	40.6	33.5	34.5	35.6
Persons: 55+	18.0	11.0	7.6	8.1	7.3

The same analysis also looked at the shifting demographic on the then social networking market leader, MySpace:

Table 7:   Demographic Profile of Visitors to MySpace.com (Lipsman, 2006a)

Demographic Profile of Visitors to MySpace.com
Percent Composition of Total Unique Visitors, August 2006 vs. August 2005
Total U.S. – Home/Work/University Locations
Source: comScore Media Metrix

| | MySpace.com Percent (%) Composition of Unique Visitors | | |
	Aug-05	Aug-06	Point Change
Unique Visitors (000)	*21,819*	*55,778*	
Total Audience	100.0	100.0	0.0
Persons: 12-17	24.7	11.9	-12.8
Persons: 18-24	19.6	18.1	-1.4
Persons: 25-34	10.4	16.7	6.2
Persons: 35-54	32.4	40.6	8.2
Persons: 55+	7.1	11.0	3.9

In September 2006, Facebook, which started as a networking site for college students, decided to open up to the public. Within less than a year, the unique monthly visitor count to the site (which had been holding steady at about 14 million) doubled, with the vast majority of growth outside the 18-24 group:

Table 8:   Facebook.com Demographic Profile (Lipsman, 2006b)

Facebook.com Demographic Profile Unique Visitors (000), May 2007 vs. May 2006 Total U.S.– Home/Work/University Locations Source: comScore Media Metrix			
	Facebook.com		
Age Segment	May-06 (000)	May-07 (000)	Percent Change
Total Audience Unique Visitors (000)	14,069	26,649	89%
Persons: 12-17	1,628	4,060	149%
Persons: 18-24	5,674	7,843	38%
Persons: 25-34	1,114	3,134	181%
Persons: 35+	5,247	10,412	98%

A growing number of sites are trying to take advantage of the increased social participation by older users, including Boomj, Boomertown, Eons, Gather, Maya's Mom, Multiply, and Rezoom (Lipsman, 2006b). Some explicitly target by age group, while others focus on specific topics that are likely to be of interest to older consumers, e.g., reading (Gather, LibraryThing), parenting (Maya's Mom, Café Mom), and personal finance (Geezeo).

The numbers tell a simple trend: Use of social technologies is widespread among youth and expanding rapidly among adults. Familiarity with the technology is often posited as a factor for usage by the older demographic, particularly business people; however, that is not sufficient to account for the wide disparity in adoption of social networking sites between older and younger users.

If we consider Maslow's hierarchy of needs, it potentially offers some insight into the generation gap. While Internet usage now crosses all class lines, it is still true that, on average, younger users come from moderately to highly affluent households. In the context of Maslow's hierarchy, their parents and school are meeting their fundamental physiological and safety needs. In fact, the willingness of so many young people to give out personally identifiable information online is evidence that safety is not a concern—they perceive that they are safe.

Michael Pokocky, Copyright © 2007

The next level of needs is love and belonging, i.e., social needs. Accordingly, online social media has become the dominant form of social interaction and entertainment among teens, and it is primarily about managing friendships, not dating and romance. A Pew Research Center study found:

- 55% of online teens have created a personal profile online, and 55% have used social networking sites like MySpace or Facebook.

- 48% of teens visit social networking websites daily or more often; 26% visit once a day, 22% visit several times a day.

- 91% of all social networking teens say they use the sites to stay in touch with friends they see frequently, while 82% use the sites to stay in touch with friends they rarely see in person.

    Chapter 13: The Age Factors

- 72% of all social networking teens use the sites to make plans with friends; 49% use the sites to make new friends.

- Just 17% of all social networking teens say they use the sites to flirt.

(Lenhart and Madden, 2007)

By contrast, when a 2007 survey of adult social networking users asked the questions, "Why do users join a social network? What is their number 1 reason?" The results were not social in nature:

A large percentage—89%—put "professional use" as their number one reason to join an online community! 53% use it to socialize and to stay connected with friends and a meager 16% is interested in joining a social network if it caters to his or her hobby. Keeping in mind the old prejudice (from people who are not using social networks obviously) that online communities are predominantly used by teenagers who like to chat (socialize), this survey stated the opposite. In addition, it makes you wonder about the surge of specialized networks (niche networks) and their chances of survival if they offer no business advantage (De Jonghe, 2007).

While we recognize that there is a significant selection bias in this survey (respondents were self-selecting, not random, and the survey was promoted primarily on business-oriented networking sites), the findings are valuable. Other surveys have had similar findings: Adult users of social networking sites are using them more for career and commerce than for just socializing (Vickers, 2007b).

It is easy to conclude that this is tied again to Maslow's hierarchy. Adoption of social networking sites has been particularly high among entrepreneurs and solo professionals versus corporate workers. Some of it is due to corporate controls: for example, approximately 50% of corporate employees do not have access to Facebook at work, as their company has blocked it (Marketing Vox, 2007). For others, the business value is simply not clear and they cannot use it for purely social purposes during work hours.

Entrepreneurs, on the other hand, not only have the freedom to use the sites at their discretion, they also use them to fill fundamental needs such as safety and health—even more fundamental than that for socialization.

Unlike students, adult heads of household are responsible for providing for the physiological needs of food and shelter, not only for themselves, but for their families as well. People who have responsibilities in that area—job seekers, business owners, solo professionals, commission-based salespeople, etc., may use social networking and social media as tools to help them meet that most basic need: making money. Conversely, workers who consider themselves in stable, tightly defined jobs—government employees, clerical workers, etc.—may not feel a compelling need to use social media.

Beyond these basic needs, adult users also look to these sites to help meet their security needs: job security, avoiding frauds and rip-offs, preventing bad decisions, etc. Once they have met their basic needs, they look for stability. Building their social network is not just a social activity; it is insurance in the event of job loss or business downturn.

According to a May 2007 survey conducted by the Institute for Corporate Productivity:

- 47% of business professionals employ social networking for professional purposes.

- Of those who use social networking technologies:

    - 71% use them to connect with former or current colleagues.

    - 55% use them to share best practices and answer questions.

    - 35% use them as an aid to finding a job.

    - 25% use them to meet customers and suppliers.

- 52% of respondents whose organizations are using social networking sites do so to keep internal staff and remote employees connected.

- 47% of total respondents use the networks to connect with potential clients and to highlight their skills.

- 35% use networks to assist them in finding a job.

- 55% of those using the networks do so to share best practices with colleagues.

- 49% use them to get answers to issues they are currently facing. (Vickers, 2007a)

Conclusion

It is clear from the many data points that there is a fundamental difference between the way young people and older adults use social software. For young people, the usage is purely social, and the primary activities are conversations or the coordination of social activities. For adults, social networking is a means to an end, whether it is finding a mate, being a better parent, personal and spiritual development, getting a job, finding new clients, or starting a business.

Companies developing services for a younger audience will want to focus on enabling communication and social connection. Those targeting an adult audience, whether consumers or B2B, should plan to include task-oriented functionality to the site, or even to have the task functionality be the focal point of the site and the social features an integral part of the application.

References

De Jonghe, A. (2007, August 1). *Survey social networks worldwide: the results.* Retrieved September 15, 2007, from www.worldwidenetworking.blogspot.com/2007/08/survey-social-net works-worldwide.html http://tinyurl.com/ypljoc

Lenhart, A. and Madden, M. (2007, January 7). *Social Networking Websites and Teens: Over half (55%) of online teens have web profiles; MySpace dominates networking world.* Retrieved October 5, 2007, from http://pewresearch.org/pubs/118/social-networking-websites-and-teens

Lipsman, A. (2006a). *More than Half of MySpace Visitors are Now Age 35 or Older, as the Site's Demographic Composition Continues to Shift.* Retrieved October 5, 2007, from http://www.comscore.com/press/release.asp?press=1019

Lipsman, A. (2006b). *Facebook Sees Flood of New Traffic From Teenagers And Adults*. Retrieved October 5, 2007, from http://www.comscore.com/press/release.asp?press=1519

Marketing Vox (2007, August 24). *Survey: Half of Employees Blocked from Facebook at Work*. Retrieved October 10, 2007, from www.marketingvox.com/archives/2007/08/24/ survey-half-of-employees-blocked-from-facebook-at-work http://tinyurl.com/yvhass

Pokocky, Michael (2007). Sketches used by permission. All rights reserved and provided with gracious permission to use by the authors of this book.

Vickers, M. (2007a, May 29). Think Online Social Networking Is Kid Stuff? Think Again, Institute for Corporate Productivity. Retrieved January 31, 2008, from http://www.i4cp.com/i4cp/news.aspx?PostId=20200

Vickers, M. (2007b, June 8). Does Social Networking Boost Productivity?, American Management Association. Retrieved January 31, 2008, from http://www.amanet.org/performance-profits/editorial.cfm?Ed=549

14 The Individual Factors

Jay T. Deragon

The Relationship Economy is affected by our personal "filters" through which we experience the world. We do not see things as they are... we see things as we are.

As individuals, it is up to us to determine how we use our social networks and how our profiles reflect the personal and professional image we desire. Our selections of networks, applications, and photographs all begin to coalesce to provide a mini portrait of us. The more we post and participate in forums and groups—the more that others gain insight into our preferences, our thoughts, and our priorities. Every keystroke we enter into the public domain is a reflection of whom we are and how we want to be perceived.

Some may remember having to turn the radio dial ever so carefully, just to get a clear channel. Now the brilliant invention—podcasting—gives us an improvement over traditional radio with digital clarity and anywhere portability. We continue to develop more uses for portable transmission every year.

Do you remember the first computers that were big enough to fill a room and had only the same limited amount of RAM as a Commodore 64?

Who could have imagined 50 or 60 years ago that computers would one day be able to compete with those behemoths and exceed their performance?

Shooting, editing and distributing video once was the sole province of large media companies (Big Media). Only Big Media could afford to reach a TV audience built in their own image. Now video is in the users' hands, and audience building by former members of the audience is alive and well on the Web. Big Media was once (exclusively) the editors of the news, choosing what ran on the front page of a publication. Now we are editors in our own right. We can edit the news and our choices, as well as send items (or have sent) to our own front pages. A highly centralized media system had connected people "up" to big social agencies and centers of power but not "across" to each other.

Right now, the horizontal flow, citizen-to-citizen, is as real and consequential as the vertical one. Noted author and media expert Dan Gillmor is involved with Harvard University and the University of California Berkeley in the Center for Citizen Media, a new initiative aimed at helping to enable and encourage grassroots media, especially citizen journalism, at every level. Gillmor's term for us, the citizens of the world is "the former audience." It refers to the owners and operators of tools that were once exclusively used by Big Media people to capture and hold our attention (Gillmor, 2004).

Jeff Jarvis (2004), a former media executive, explained the trend in peoples' use of media. "Give the people control of media, they will use it," Jarvis said. "The corollary: Don't give the people control of media, and you will lose. Whenever citizens can exercise control, they will" (Jarvis, 2004).

Tom Glocer, CEO of Reuters Group, also recognized the trend: "If you want to attract a community around you, you must offer them something original and of a quality that they can react to and incorporate in their creative work" (Rosen, 2006).

Now media is beginning to understand the implications. They are learning from us and from our business associates as they begin to observe and describe the same shifts.

   Chapter 14: The Individual Factors

"We already own the eyeballs on the television screen. We want to make sure we own the eyeballs on the computer screen," said Ann Kirschner (as cited in Rosen, 2006), Former Vice President of Programming and Media Development for the National Football League.

Glocer, Jarvis, Kirschner, and a host of others should know that such delusions as "we own the eyeballs" were the historical products of a media system that gave its operators an exaggerated sense of their own power and mastery over others.

How do we capitalize on the shifting economy? By Branding. Each one of us needs to **brand ourselves personally**.

Management guru and author Tom Peters clearly "gets it":

> Regardless of age, regardless of position, regardless of the business we happen to be in, all of us need to understand the importance of branding. We are the CEOs of our own companies: Me, Inc. You're not defined by your job title and you're not confined by your job description. So what defines you? (Peters, 2000).

Garr Reynolds, Associate Professor of Management at Kansai Gaidai University and former Manager of Worldwide User Group Relations at Apple Computer, understands what it takes to succeed in The Relationship Economy.

"The greatest brands of all—that is, the greatest brands to you—are much like a trusted friend. In a sense, we judge brands by asking ourselves the same kind of questions we would ask about people we know or are thinking of doing business with," Reynolds said (Reynolds, 2004).

For example, we might ask: Is he authentic? Is he reliable? Is he honest? Can we trust him? Does he make me feel better about myself? The bonds we have with our most trusted friends are bonds based on a promise. Our relationships with brands are not (usually) as strong as those with people. Of course, if a brand breaks a promise, customers will feel betrayed, angry, and take their business elsewhere. Great brands have distinct personalities and people usually choose brands that match their own unique personalities and individualism.

Peter Montoya's book *The Personal Branding Phenomenon* is characterized in its marketing description as: "It's the new reality no one wants to concede—and it's the cold, hard reality behind success in the new millennium. From the schoolroom to the boardroom, everyone succeeds—or fails—by the rules of Personal Branding." (Amazon.co.jp, 2007)

Personal branding is not the product of ad agencies or corporations; it is a continuous process that is as old as society. A personal brand—the values, abilities, and personality traits people associate with each of us—affects our careers, our relationships…our lives.

You have two choices: Surrender to the process, or seize control of it. Consider how much social networking and related emerging technology is creating the phenomena of individual branding. Our brand is largely influenced by what and how we communicate, to whom we are connected to as well as where our presence is throughout the worldwide Web.

Soon it will not matter which existing network you think is better, rather the value will be created by how you manage your network. As more and more closed systems open, they begin to interact more directly with other existing systems, and therefore acquire all the value of those systems.

Technology provides the means, **relationships provide the value**.

Here are seven things to consider and help you start thinking and planning for "your" network:

- Which networks do you want fed to your network? Which has your interest, value, the best collection of individuals and the content that matches with who you are?

- Which networks represent your interests geographically, by industry and by topic? Which blogs represent the same categories of interest?

- What will be the rules of your network? Standards for connections? RSS feeds in and out?

- **What image and brand do you want your network to project?**

- What media do you want in your network? Video, audio, pictures, etc. What network channels will be available that interest you most both personally and professionally?

- What do you specifically want to accomplish with your network?

- Your network is an economic factory. How do you produce quality and quantity effectively?

In the very near future, we will all be overwhelmed with an abundance of value propositions in which you'll need to decide how and what to use in your network to meet your personal and professional goals. You will be in charge of your brand, your public persona. In addition, you will soon become your own aggregator of networks, of relationships, of information, of knowledge, and last but not least…of value.

References

Amazon.co.jp. (2007). Retrieved November 20, 2007, from www.amazon.co.jp/Personal-Branding-Phenomenon-Influence-Advancement/dp/0967450616 http://tinyurl.com/2vfhjv

Gillmor, D. (2004). *We the Media—Grassroots Journalism by the People, for the People.* Retrieved October 12, 2007, from http://www.authorama.com/book/we-the-media.html

Jarvis, J. (2004, November 13). *The third axis of media: Medium, message ... and messenger.* Retrieved October 5, 2007, from http://www.buzzmachine.com/archives/2004_11_13.html#008475

Montoya, P. (2002). *The Personal Branding Phenomenon.* Tustin, CA: Peter Montoya, Inc.

Peters, T. (2000). *The Brand You 50: Fifty Ways to Transform Yourself from an 'Employee' into a Brand That Shouts Distinction, Commitment, and Passion.* New York: Random House.

Reynolds, G. (2004). *Branding: Brands are personal.* Retrieved October 10, 2007, from http://www.garrreynolds.com/Branding/index.html

Rosen, J. (2006, June 27). The People Formerly Known as the Audience. *Press Think.* Retrieved October 15, 2007, from www.journalism.nyu.edu/pubzone/weblogs/pressthink/2006/06/27/ppl_frmr.html http://tinyurl.com/nh5oc

15 The Relationship Capital Factors

Adam J. Kovitz*

Every day The Relationship Economy evolves and progresses, yet most people are not aware of the subtle changes taking place. And while the iterative versions of this emerging economy are certainly far from perfect, then again, so is our current economic system—yet we've been looking for ways to live within and capitalize upon it for decades.

We have been dependent on monetary policies for the transfer of goods and services. We have used commodities, buyer spending habits, forecasting techniques, interest rates, and trade deficits and surpluses as some indicators to determine fiscal policy and financial strength. Each nation is affected when it does business with other countries and participates in their economies.

Monetary and trade policy affects many; sometimes for the better, sometimes otherwise. We like to think that such decisions are made for

---

* *Adam J. Kovitz is Founder and Publisher of* **The National Networker,** *and is the Executive Director of the Relationship Networking Industry Association (RNIA).*

the betterment of the majority or for the financial stability of the corporation or country. However, not everyone is the beneficiary of every policy, and in the high-speed, hyper-linked world of The Relationship Economy, where everyone has an equal voice and quantity means influence, traditional policies can have serious and unintended consequences.

Competition vs. Cooperation

Our current economy is based on the concept of "healthy competition." In the past, we justified competition as a motivator and way to ensure forward progress. The downside to this is that there are always losers, and their numbers continue to swell as the benefits go to the "survival of the fittest" (or at least the well connected). In the end, there is only one survivor who has everything. This creates an unhealthy paradigm, as people at the top do not stay in that position for very long.

What is so intriguing about The Relationship Economy and its centerpiece, relationship capital, is that it promises so much more than the traditional "I win, you lose" ideology that is inherent in the current economy. The Relationship Economy takes into account that even the most rugged individualists who yearn for independence, at the end of the day, still remain interdependent upon one another. Therefore, the "win-win" model of cooperation built into Relationship Capital states in the end that no one wins unless everyone wins.

A Definition

The Relationship Networking Industry Association (RNIA) defines relationship capital as a "measure of the perceptions inherent in the internal and external interactions among people, products and organizations. Its value is tallied throughout and beyond the lifetime of the subject being measured" (Relationship Networking Industry Association, 2007).

          Chapter 15: The Relationship Capital Factors

Why Now?

The concept of relationship capital seems relatively controversial, subversive, utopian, or even revolutionary at times, when one explores the implications of the Laws of Relationship Capital. For those proponents of relationship capital and The Relationship Economy, the time is certainly now to gain support. Several factors are influencing decisions at this time:

- The United States, one of the world's top economic powers, is currently experiencing an erosion of the middle class (Ehrenreich and Draut, 2006), weakening dollar (Bajaj and Austen, 2007), and record-breaking debt (CBS News, 2007). Authors Donald Trump and Robert Kyosaki suggest that the 20 percent of Americans controlling 80% of the wealth is actually shrinking to 10 percent controlling ninety (Trump and Kyosaki, 2006).

- In their book *The Cluetrain Manifesto*, Rick Levine, Christopher Locke, Doc Searls, and David Weinberger (2000) speak to the point that Markets are Conversations. Their point supports that growing, widespread use of the Internet is facilitating conversations that defy the traditional boundaries of corporations and countries. In time, these conversations can become movements that affect corporate and even national policies. At the center of these Internet conversations are Web 2.0 technologies and the online utilities that use them. These technologies are now being adopted and acquired by many large organizations such as IBM, Disney, Coca Cola, and Google, just to name a few.

- The Millennials, otherwise known as "Generation Y," born between 1982 and 2002, are entering the workforce. This generation, according to experts, is one of the most misunderstood of all time as they are non-linear in thinking, highly principled, highly adaptive to new technology and well connected, especially online. Unlike previous generations, there is a tendency to place less value on money and more on connections, knowledge and freedom of expression (Degraffenreid, 2006 and 2007).

- Academia, corporations, and other insiders are researching the unprecedented confluence of technology, relationship networking, education, media, sociology and gaming.

- Educational institutions are receiving grant money to research relationship networking and implement new workshops, courses, and curricula (NSFA, 2007).

- The events of September 11, 2001, served as a symbolic attack on the U.S.-supported capitalist system, hitting both the financial center of New York as well as the political/military center in Washington, DC. The aftermath has caused many around the globe to re-think their humanity in terms both practical and esoteric (Schwarz, 2004).

The Wild West

As these factors play into the emergence of both the relationship networking industry and The Relationship Economy, a global paradigm shift is happening. This shift is causing new, vast exploration. Pragmatically speaking, corporations and entrepreneurs are beginning to look at ways to capitalize upon this, but there is a certain element of the "Wild West" out there. There are no applicable laws in place as governments scramble to understand the impact on national security that online networking poses (Marks, 2006). At the same time, corporations must deal with issues of whether their employees should spend time on sites like MySpace, LinkedIn, and Facebook (Hoover, 2007).

A Closer Look at the Laws of Relationship Capital

While there is still a lot of confusion about the brave new world of The Relationship Economy, there have been some initial attempts to establish order to the growing chaos. One is the Relationship Networking Industry Association (RNIA), a non-profit association that, through its members, is amassing a Common Body of Knowledge (CBOK) of best practices and standards. The second is the ten Laws of Relationship Capital. They address who can possess Relationship Capital, where it comes from, how it is valuated, how it changes, and how it relates to both Intellectual and Financial Capital.

                    Chapter 15: The Relationship Capital Factors

The First Law:

All organic entities (living or at one time having lived) possess and have the potential to create relationship capital.

What the First Law states is that all beings defined under the biological taxonomy of kingdoms—animals (including humans), plants, bacteria, etc.—possess relationship capital. Even more intriguing is that our relationship capital remains even after we are gone, and is valued upon our legacy. Therefore, wood, oil, fossils and food also contain relationship capital.

To this extent, figures from our history such as Benjamin Franklin, Karl Marx, Julius Caesar, Queen Elizabeth the First, and Adolf Hitler all possess relationship capital. Additionally, fossilized dinosaur bones and plant life possess relationship capital, because through understanding their nature, we can better define humanities role in the universe.

The First Law also brings a new perspective to the various sciences and "ologies" in our world. As we construct an entity relationship matrix of the various kingdoms of biological taxonomy, living and otherwise, we begin to see that sociology, anthropology, ecology, paleontology, archeology, and history are all studies of how humans and other organisms relate to one another. This even leaves a placeholder for the study of the paranormal. And while such a matrix suggests that there are branches of study out there that have yet to be discovered, such branches probably have not been discovered because there is little practical application or relevance.

The First Law even gives new meaning to birth. The question that is posed is: "How does one value the relationship capital of an infant?" Most likely, it will have to do with a composite of the parents' relationship capital. However, this also raises another question: "Do children born into privilege possess more relationship capital than those who do not?" Most likely, this is the case. Either way, it will be interesting to see a time when a birth announcement will contain the relationship capital value at birth along with height and weight.

The Second Law:

Non-organic entities do not possess relationship capital, but reflect the collective relationship capital of those relationship capital-possessing entities that have relationships with them.

The Second Law pertains to all other entities that do not fall under the biological taxonomy: inorganic entities, with which we may still have relationships, even though they cannot possess relationship capital. The controversy over this law is based on the argument that we can have relationships with cars, computers and toasters—why cannot they possess relationship capital?

The answer is that practically, value can be placed upon any non-organic material product, but should be based upon the relationship capital imbued upon it by others who possess it. This is similar to the way a painting is valued, based upon the perceived value of the work by the artist, not upon the materials used. Of course, many non-organic products are valued by the materials in them—consider luxury items such as Rolex watches.

No matter which side of the organic/non-organic argument prevails, the intent of the First and Second Laws are to place organic entities at the height of The Relationship Economy food chain.

The Third Law:

Relationship Capital is derived from the collective relationships an individual has with other relationship capital-possessing entities.

The Third Law states that when we aggregate the many relationships we have with other relationship capital-possessing entities on an individual basis, we derive an overall relationship capital value for an individual.

The implications here are that part of the valuation for organic entities depends upon perceived value. The components of such a perceived value include:

- The way the individual in question perceives the relationship (possibly as simple as on a scale of 1 to 10).

- The way the Relationship capital-possessing entity perceives the relationship with the individual in question.

- Commonly accepted practices and standards.

As organizations like RNIA continue to develop the metrics by which relationship capital is measured, separate formulas might be developed to distinguish the methods of valuation for organic vs. non-organic entities. Considerations for valuation of non-organic relationship capital might include:

- Relationship capital value of those who produce the item.

- Intellectual capital value (see the Seventh and Eighth Laws) relevant to the product or service.

- Time and research invested into the product or service.

- Materials used.

- Commonly accepted practices and standards.

Case in point: Would you buy a new software product produced through a joint venture of Bill Gates and Steve Jobs or through the joint venture of John Smith and Mary Jones? Most people would choose the former because of demonstrated dominance and credibility in the software space, whereas the latter choice is unknown.

Localized effects also influence relationship capital value. For example, Osama Bin Laden may have a relatively strong negative relationship capital value on the world stage, but within Al Qaida circles, it would surely be quite the opposite.

The Fourth Law:

Relationship capital value increases or decreases proportionally as the perceived quality of relationship increases or decreases.

The Fourth Law suggests that relationship capital value can exist in three states:

1. **Positive**—The entity is respected, trusted, loved and/or highly useful to many, can be an asset to an organization and supports survival, or

2. **Negative**—The entity is hated, has a reputation of being untrustworthy and/or poisonous to many, can be a detriment to an organization and supports destruction, or

3. **Neutral (zero)**—The entity is unknown, unrecognized, brand new, irrelevant, inert or forgotten.

The Fourth Law implies a time element to relationship capital, of which the relationship capital value can change, either positively or negatively. For example, a relationship timeline might start with two entities as complete strangers (relationship capital value is zero), becoming the closest of friends (relatively high positive value), having a fallout (negative value), losing touch with each other for a long time (back to zero), and suddenly running into each other after years, putting aside their differences.

Another implication of this Law includes the concept of *relationship inertia,* wherein the longer and/or stronger relationship capital value tends to be positive or negative, the longer it will most likely remain there. For example, if Person A saves Person B's life, the relationship capital value would tend to be strongly positive, as it has great impact. It would be much harder to swing the relationship capital value negative (localized to this particular relationship), even if Person A forgot Person B's birthday or to return their phone call.

The Fifth Law:

Relationship capital can never be destroyed.

The good news implied in the Fifth Law is that relationship capital is eternal. However, that relationship capital cannot be measured and is considered inert or zero if an individual has no historically recorded history. This can be good news for relationship capital-possessing entities that have had a negative relationship capital score.

We have evidence of continuing relationship capital value both in real life and in fictional stories. For example, an ancient being encased in ice and forgotten until they are recovered has had a positive or negative relationship capital value that was rendered inert for a long period of time, only to be recovered and brought back to a positive or negative value.

The Fifth Law also implies that all relationship capital value has the potential, over time, to go to zero. The way to preserve positive or negative relationship capital value is through communications that have been historically recorded and left retrievable trails: traditional mail, email, blogging, networking, books, propaganda, rhetoric, campaigns, etc.

Because relationship capital can only be created and not destroyed, this created a potential downside to relationship capital: the eminent threat of inflation. Experts suggest that one of the best ways to deal with this is to employ select portions of relationship capital that have an expiration date.

The Sixth Law:

Relationship capital of an organization is the aggregate of the individual relationship capital of its constituents.

The Sixth Law ties relationship capital to organizational dynamics; that is, the collective relationship capital of all members (employees, constituents, and customers) comprises the total relationship capital of the whole, and is useful in evaluating organizational effectiveness in terms of management, M&A, the stock market, etc. It also refers to an organization of relatively strong relationship capital value (positive or negative) due to some exceptional combination of members, plan, process, branding, or outreach.

One major implication of the Sixth Law is that individuals do not have relationships in the sense of relationship capital with an organization, but rather, with the individuals who represent the organization. It is also important to note that an organization is a synergistic group of one or more individuals and therefore, the term is interchangeable and synonymous with "company," "country," "network," "political party," "society," "clan," "caste," "club," "team," etc.

The valuation of organizational relationship capital is based on the following:

- Combined relationship capital of all entities (organic and non-organic) comprising the organization, including members, contractors, assets, and liabilities.

- Combined intellectual capital of all entities comprising the organization, including but not limited to:

  - Vision of company

  - Mission of company

  - Copyrights, Patents, Trademarks

  - Branding

  - Supporting Processes

- Level of actions taken by members relative to organizational vision and mission (alignment).

- The way outside relationship capital-possessing entities (customers, environment) perceive the relationship with the organization.

The Seventh Law:

Intellectual capital can only be created by one or more relationship capital-possessing entities.

Intellectual property is understood in concept, highly sought after, highly disputed in courts of law, and used for competitive advantage. It can also be valuated—hence the term "Intellectual Capital." This, in itself, is a field of study that is beyond the scope of this book.

The importance of the Seventh Law is really a statement of the obvious—relationship capital-possessing entities are the source of intellectual capital. This again, stresses the sovereignty of organic over non-organic entities and conceptual entities.

The Seventh Law also underscores the fact that both relationship capital and intellectual capital are both forms of capital and can be related to, exchanged for, and valuated at some amount of currency or medium of exchange.

The Eighth Law:

Conceptual entities such as brands, services, and inventions, which possess intellectual capital, can be leveraged like non-organic entities to reflect, store, amplify and/or negate relationship capital. Therefore, intellectual capital is a tool for modifying relationship capital.

When we think of brands and/or concepts like Coca Cola, Nike, or even Communism, we immediately have a reaction on both conscious and unconscious levels. The intellectual capital (as well as the relationship capital) that went into such concepts affects us either positively or negatively. Therefore, individuals, despite their own personal relationship capital who represent such concepts may be overshadowed due to the "power" of those concepts when looking to influence others. Consequently, the individual on the other end would be affected either positively or negatively in regard to the representative—this happens all the time in the world of sales and marketing.

The same can be said with services (such as financial planning, life insurance, and abortion), inventions (rubber, cars, and guns), and fictional characters (Superman, Garfield, Darth Vader, and Santa Claus). Each of these entities has been imbued over the years with both intellectual and relationship capital by their creators, believers, promoters, supporters and critics.

The Ninth Law:

Financial capital is merely a reflection of and cannot exist without some combination of relationship and intellectual capital.

The Ninth Law states that the financial capital that we use in our current economy to pay our bills, pay for our education, and to invest and plan for our retirement is not possible without relationship and intellectual capital. This also implies that financial capital is illusory at best and does not properly reflect the true nature (and value) of organic entities. In fact, when over-stressed or over-emphasized, financial capital mitigates the usefulness of the relationship capital-possessing entities that produce it, causing a downward spiral effect that results in reduced production of all forms of capital.

Consider this scenario: A person who lost his or her parent in an accident forms a new company to produce accident-preventing widgets that will save the lives of billions of people. The founder is obviously motivated and builds exceptionally high levels of relationship capital. The company grows out of his or her garage an into a small office building with one hundred employees who are happy and highly motivated.

A larger corporation looking to expand its product lines contacts the owner about buying the company. The owner believes that they can take the company farther (and quicker) with an infusion of capital and expertise, and decides to accept the offer, staying on board as the director of the newly established corporate division.

Unfortunately, due to "creative differences" and corporate politics, the former owner-turned-director is ousted from the company he or she started and a new director—a long-time company man—is brought in as a replacement. Relationship capital value begins to slide because the employees who were loyal to the former owner begin to miss the small-time family feel of the organization and begin to quit, taking their relationship and intellectual capital with them. New employees are brought in from elsewhere in the corporation, but lack the original passion that drove this company forward.

In time, the division begins to lose money. Budgets are cut. New directors come and go. There is a major initiative to find ways to cut costs, including those in the manufacturing of the widgets. Jobs are lost. Customers who have had great relationships with some of the "old regulars" in customer service are working with people who are either incompetent or uncaring. Relationship capital value is sinking fast but no one notices as they are watching the company's stock price plummet. Eventually, the division is closed or sold to someone who can revitalize the company.

Like the saying goes, "It's about the relationships, stupid!" The most effective companies who understand and implement this concept will thrive in The Relationship Economy.

The other implication here is that financial capital changes, in time, as relationship and intellectual capital change, and is directly proportional unless there is a corruption of the system, which brings us to…

The Tenth Law:

Relationship and intellectual capital always conform to the laws of nature and humankind. Financial capital does not...necessarily.

Again, over-emphasis on financial capital ultimately negates the significance of people, and leads (often out of desperation) to keeping and protecting secrets. Systems like this produce corruption where few "succeed" at the cost of many.

The Tenth Law suggests that relationship and intellectual capital tend to be self-regulating systems that take advantage of populism, either in the form of the Internet or other media. In a populist medium, the system is much more difficult to corrupt as everyone watches each other. In a pure relationship economy, there are no secrets and no places to hide, as everyone is held accountable. It is only through co-operation and collaboration that the whole moves forward in a positive direction.

The Impact of the Laws

The laws of relationship capital suggest a new approach to business as well as the way we view the world, in general. Introducing these laws is expected to spark debate, conversation, awareness as well as further research—including new fields of study. The laws of relationship capital are not set in stone and are subject to change as social network science evolves; nevertheless, they are a closest approximation to our understanding of the universe today.

About the Contributing Author

Adam J. Kovitz is Founder and Publisher of *The National Networker (TNNW)*, a free online magazine with a blog and its own podcasting channel. He also serves as the Executive Director of the Relationship Networking Industry Association (RNIA), which is a non-profit association whose vision is to facilitate a seamlessly-connected Relationship Economy. In addition, he writes a monthly column for TNNW and is heard weekly on *The National Networker Show.*

References

Bajaj, V. and Austen, I. (2007, September 21). Dollar falls to new low Against the Euro. *The New York Times.* Retrieved October 5, 2007, from www.nytimes.com/2007/09/21/business/worldbusiness/21dollar.html http://tinyurl.com/3xxjl8

CBS News (2007, January 7). *Record High Consumer Debt.* Retrieved October 10, 2007 from http://www.youtube.com/watch?v=2N0NHu2GJm8

Degraffenreid, S. (2006 and 2007). *Resistance is Futile! Millennials Hit the Workforce* and *Getting Gamers: Painting the Target!* Retrieved April 24, 2007, from http://www.necessarymeasures.com

Ehrenreich, B. and Draut, T. (2006, October 16). *Downsized but Not Out,* Retrieved October 5, 2007, from http://www.thenation.com/doc/20061106/ehrenreich

Hoover, J. N. (2007, September 27). Social Networking: A Time Waster or the Next Big Thing in Collaboration? *InformationWeek.* Retrieved October 5, 2007 from www.informationweek.com/news/showArticle.jhtml?articleID=201808149 http://tinyurl.com/2qdek8

Levine, R., Locke, C., Searls, D., and Weinberger, D. (2000). *The Cluetrain Manifesto: The End of Business as Usual.* New York: Perseus Books.

Marks, P. (2006, June 9). Pentagon Sets its Sights on Social Networking Websites. *NewScientist.* Retrieved October 5, 2007, from http://www.newscientist.com/article/mg19025556.200.html

NSFA - National Science Foundation Award #0633401. (2007,
March 8). *Theoretical and Applied Approaches to Teaching Social
Computing in STEM Education.* Retrieved October 13, 2007, from
www.nsf.gov/awardsearch/showAward.do?AwardNumber=0633401
http://tinyurl.com/3botc4

Relationship Networking Industry Association. Retrieved October 5,
2007, from http://www.rnia.org

Schwarz, J. (2004, September 23). *Americans had Strong Need for
Spiritual Support Following 9/11 Attacks.* Retrieved October 10, 2007,
from http://uwnews.washington.edu/ni/article.asp?articleID=5611

Trump, D. J. and Kyosaki, R. T. (2006). *Why We Want You to Be Rich.*
New York: Rich Press.

16 | The Us Factors

Jay T. Deragon

Few, if any of us, live in isolation. When we find individuals who do choose to live in isolation, the outcomes appear sad to us and we wonder why. All of us interact with others for numerous personal and professional reasons. These interactions shape our world and influence our individual emotions, perspective, spirit, and identity. For The Relationship Economy, "The Us Factors" are an identity that individuals create for themselves through their online social interactions, which produce deflections and affective meaning for their identity.

Social networks accelerate social interactions. Social interaction is a dynamic, changing sequence of social actions between individuals (or groups) that modify their actions and reactions according to the actions by their interaction partner(s) (Social interaction, 2007). In short, social interactions are events through which people attach meaning to a situation, interpret what others mean, and respond accordingly.

Michael Pokocky, Copyright © 2007

Social interactions can be differentiated as:

- **Accidental** (also known as social contact)—not planned and likely not repeated. Examples of accidental social interactions would include asking a stranger for directions or a shopkeeper for product availability (Social contact, 2007).

- **Repeated**—not planned, bound to happen from time to time. An example of a repeated social interaction would include meeting a neighbor from time to time when walking on your street.

- **Regular**—not planned, but very common, likely to raise questions when missed. Examples of regular social interactions would include meeting a door attendant or a security guard every workday in your workplace, dining every day in the same restaurant, etc.

- **Regulated**—planned and regulated by customs or law, will definitely raise questions when missed. Examples of regulated social interactions would include interaction in a workplace or with family.

　　　　　　　　　　　　　　Chapter 16: The Us Factors

Interaction comes naturally to many people, but some may misunderstand the power inherent in such a simple and natural activity. Though at first it may seem that many relationships barely scratch the surface, they often strengthen exponentially as we develop more (and more important) connections with those in our social networks. These stronger relationships are needed to support the growing network, and they, in turn, attract others to the network.

These relationships are formed based on a static exchange of communications, which identifies each individual's interest and affinities. It is initially from this exposure to each other's interest and affinities, and subsequently from learning more about the interests we share with others, that we each individually become a part of the common "us" in the virtual world of networking. The medium of online social networks creates new meaning in the sociological hierarchy. The meaningful information we share drives us to find more ways and reasons to collaborate, connect, share and learn together as a community. The concept of community is taking new form in The Relationship Economy.

When we build relationships, we start out with definable concepts that ultimately transform into impressions of others. The Evaluation, Potency, and Activity (EPA) scale (Affect Control Theory, 2007) demonstrates the affective meanings that fluctuate across three dimensions:

- **Evaluation**—goodness versus badness

- **Potency**—powerfulness versus powerlessness

- **Activity**—liveliness versus torpidity

Semantic differentials, which measure the connotative meaning of concepts (Semantic Differential, 2007), can be used to measure these affective meanings by indicating how the concept is positioned on the scale.

People have been describing each other since they developed the ability to speak (Semantic Differential, 2007). Though we may not openly describe each other, the process occurs, nonetheless. In this comprehensive, often reactive description, the basic perceptions of each other exist, such as relative height, weight, and appearance. However, the more we get to know each other, the more likely we are to add descriptions like *trustworthy, supportive, fun.* As the description process progresses, the strength of the bonds between us change. These changing bonds (connections) affect our networks in ways that are often difficult to understand.

A stable affective meaning derived from either personal experience or cultural affect is called a sentiment, or a fundamental affective meaning (Affect Control Theory, 2007). These affective meanings may conflict with the sentiments or perceptions of others, in turn, affecting our relationships and the strength of our network connections; but to us they are accurate.

The effect of sentiment on our networks must be understood if we are to successfully build—and ultimately contribute to—the strength of our social networks. Affect control theory has inspired massive dictionaries of EPA sentiments for thousands of concepts involved in social life: identities, behaviors, settings, personal attributes, and emotions (Affect Control Theory, 2007). According to Heise (2001), affect control theory has been used in research on emotions, gender, social structure, politics, deviance and law, the arts, and business.

Additionally, sentiment dictionaries have been constructed with ratings from the U.S.A., Canada, Northern Ireland, Germany, Japan, and China (both the People's Republic and Taiwan) (Heise, 2001). The complications anticipated in the collection of so many descriptors can be overwhelming. Is all this necessary?

The players in individual social networks and related activities determine (or at least guide the choice of) the sentiments that the individual tries to maintain. Sentiments within a social network also create impressions of the person performing an action (actor), the object person, the behavior, the setting, and the relationships between all of these. Ignoring this inter-relationship may indicate to those with whom we are connected that the individual relationship is insignificant. That would lead quickly to a weakening of the bonds in the network, and ultimately, a weakened network.

As our networks grow, it is imperative that we ensure some kind of agreement can be reached on a variety of levels. Each concept that is in play in a situation has a transient affective meaning in addition to other associated sentiments. The transient meaning corresponds to an impression created by recent events, and these events modify impressions on all three EPA dimensions in a variety of complex ways (Affect Control Theory, 2007).

Here are two examples of impression-formation processes.

- A participant in online social networks who behaves disagreeably seems less worthy of social acceptance by the community good, especially if the object of the behavior is innocent and powerless, like a child or the patience for child like behavior is low.

- A powerful person seems desperate when performing extremely forceful acts on another, particularly if the community perceives the recipient as less powerful.

Individual impressions are driven by numerous elements of individual affiliations, communications, and behavior. Individual impressions cause and affect collective impressions, and both serve to strengthen (or weaken) the bonds between all of the connections in our networks.

Confirming sentiments associated with institutional identities—such as doctor-patient, lawyer-client, or professor-student—creates institutionally relevant role behavior (Affect Control Theory, 2007). Online social networks are becoming institutions of virtual relationships that collectively create swarms of institutional identities, like the groups we belong to in virtual communities, the causes we support, the networks or groups we join, etc. As we expand the types of connections, we must understand the dynamics of change relative to the sentiments and connections that affect each relationship.

Our relationships with others are often affected by events that occur between or including others. An event generates emotions for the individuals involved in the event by changing the impressions they have of others, those who have experienced similar events, and many other things related to the event. The emotion we experience is a function of the impression created in the individual and the difference between that impression and the sentiment attached to it (Affect Control Theory, 2007). Thus, for example, an event that creates a negative impression generates an unpleasant emotion for that person, and the unpleasantness is worse if the individual believes they have a highly valued identity. Similarly, an event creating a positive impression generates a pleasant emotion, which is all the more pleasant if the individual believes they have (or had) a disvalued identity in the situation or a social network. In online social networks, the determining predictive factors for individuals are found in their communications, affinity to others, activities and group associations.

The sentiment associated with an identity can change to befit the kinds of events in which that identity is involved. This is particularly true when situations arise where the identity is deflected in the same way and when identities are informal and non-institutionalized (Heise, 2007). With the emergence of social networking, much has been written about employers' screening of individuals (either employees or potential employees) using the individual's online social networking activities as a profiling tool for assessment. Such activity is creating a new science of sentiments associated with individual online activities, connections, communications and affiliations. The population of adults and youth participating in today's online social networks has no idea that their activities and related behavioral sentiments associated with their online activities can likely be used as a means for profiling for positive or less noble reasons.

Conclusion

"The Us Factors" are driven by the identity we create in the virtual world of social networks. Our subsequent behaviors and affiliations group us into social hierarchies that can be defined by computer driven mathematical engines used to create taxonomies of social sentiments, which identify us. These taxonomies can then be used for numerous reasons, good and bad, depending on the objective of usage. These methodologies are already in existence and used for numerous purposes.

As The Relationship Economy emerges, the economic transactions will create sentiments associated with our economic transactions (financial sentiments) and further define our identity. Privacy and security will become the overriding issues with which we will leverage the media to our individual benefits. One thing is certain, as the adoption curve of social networking continues to grow at exponential levels, the need for privacy and security must be addressed before the social media and its technology can be used to transform our world.

References

Affect Control Theory. (2007, October 2). Retrieved October 26, 2007, from http://en.wikipedia.org/w/index.php?title=Affect_Control_Theory

Heise, D. R. (2001). *Affect Control Theory.* Retrieved October 25, 2007, from http://www.indiana.edu/~socpsy/ACT

Heise, D. R. (2007). *Expressive Order: Confirming Sentiments in Social Actions.* New York: Springer.

Pokocky, Michael (2007). Sketches used by permission. All rights reserved and provided with gracious permission to use by the authors of this book.

Semantic differential. (2007, October 26). Retrieved October 26, 2007, from http://en.wikipedia.org/w/index.php?title=Semantic_differential

Social contact. (2007, October 9). Retrieved October 26, 2007, from http://en.wikipedia.org/w/index.php?title=Social_contact

Social interaction. (2007, September 14). Retrieved October 26, 2007, from http://en.wikipedia.org/w/index.php?title=Social_interaction

17 The Political Factors

Jay T. Deragon

With the backlash of Facebook's 2006 launch of new mini-feeds, which sent email to users' entire friends lists indicating what groups they were joining, one aspect of the political factors of social networking became evident. Users of social networking sites are willing to join forces and demand changes, including a return to the status quo when changes are made to social networking protocols. In fact, it was only time before the other political aspects fell into place.

The September 2006 launch of Facebook's mini-feeds was a call to action for Ben Parr, a junior at Northwestern University in Chicago, who created a group on Facebook called Students Against Facebook News Feed, or SANF. Within only hours after its creation, the group's membership had grown in numbers upwards of 13,000, and did not stop until reaching well above three-quarters of a million members (Schmidt, 2006).

The members of SANF signed a petition protesting these new applications and constantly blogged their thoughts about having their every move tracked and broadcast across the entire network. Just 24 hours after the new application launched, Facebook executives knew trouble was brewing based on the content of blog posts from SANF's members, which came to an estimated 90,000. That was an average of just over one new member of the group per second, every second of every hour of that day.

By joining social networking sites, *we*, the people, begin creating the news; we, the people, are the ones who are generating waves of change; we, the people, are the constituents the politicians want to reach, and we, the people on the social networks, have the means and the venue to do all of these things! Social networks are the best way to further a cause—because like-minded individuals are going to be listening to what others in their networks are saying.

In order to do this with the greatest amount of efficiency, we first need to develop our own relationship economy. Within your network, you have the ability to spread your news and instigate a call to action virally. It may start out slowly, but if each person who sees your message invites ten others to join the cause, then you have thousands of potential supporters.

Think about politicians. What better way to generate buzz around yourself than with a network? Newsweek Business suggested social networking space as possibly the next best thing on the campaign trail (Gross, 2006). Presidential hopefuls Howard Dean, John Kerry, and others were on the cusp of the Web 2.0 trend before the 2004 election, and others have followed suit (Hindo, 2004). Political organizers are urging the young adults to get out and vote, and with social networks in place, their aims can be achieved quickly and easily.

With elections in 2008 and beyond in the United States, for example, campaign directors need new ways to rally voters. Scott Heiferman, the CEO of Meetup.com, the pioneering social-networking site that helped give Howard Dean early momentum in the 2004 presidential campaign, predicts social networks will soon eclipse television in terms of impact on politics: "Expect candidates to be on millions of MySpace and Facebook buddy lists, for sure. It's a big thing, a real populist revolution." Still, Heiferman believes political networking only reaches its full effectiveness when users take the next step: meeting in person. "People need to use the Internet to get off the Internet," he says. (Meetups in the News!, 2006)

However, political advisor Sanford Dickert believes that politicians will never really invest in social networks because of their perception of low return on investment of time (man-hours)—with the one exception:

> But I make one caveat—the only way social networks will have some REAL impact will be if campaigns dedicate the energy/resources to make them effective OR to let their supporters within these networks have REAL control over the messages in a fashion as described as virtual precinct captains (Dickert, 2006).

In The Relationship Economy, social networks are the means by which we, the people, can let our voices be heard and be heard loudly. Social networks give us the ability to become informed and insightful regarding the issues about which we feel most passionately. With the advent of Web 2.0, we are able to collaborate with others to flush out ideas and then broadly cast them to a worldwide audience.

As Ben Parr demonstrated with the Facebook controversy, by initiating petitions requiring little more of the "signer" than a few mouse-clicks, we can allow our views to gain momentum, creating a synergistic effect. The more people who realize what is most important to a given population, the more likely that population may gain significant numbers of supporters and support from others.

Web 2.0 technologies allow the user, whomever it may be, to create a "platform" on which to debate hot topics and issues. All one needs is a webcam and an Internet connection. How much easier can it be to get your voice heard by millions?

On the other side of the coin, politicians can reach the people more easily and cost-effectively than ever before. The members of social networking sites are inclined to "feel a connection" to a politician because they are in the same network.

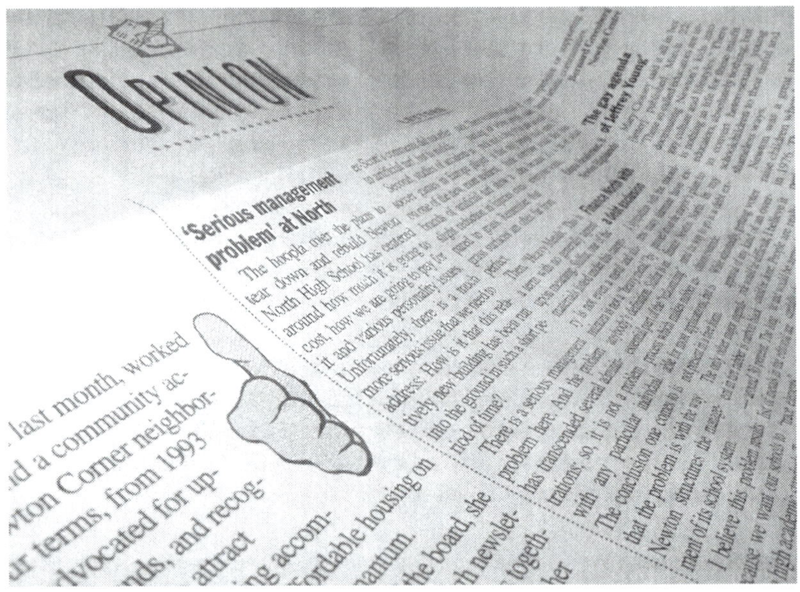

In an article in The Christian Science Monitor titled, "Web 2.0 meets Campaign 2008," Linda Feldmann observed that James Kotecki, a Georgetown University student had a one-on-one with presidential hopeful Ron Paul in his dorm room:

> Viewers will see the first-ever interview with a presidential candidate from a college dorm room. They can hear Mr. Paul present his libertarian take on foreign policy, economics, and the Constitution. In the background, the clutter of toiletries atop Mr. Kotecki's dresser adds to the "just dropping by" feel.

> (Feldmann, 2007; Kotecki, 2007)

     Chapter 17: The Political Factors

Though it is doubtful that Kotecki will be able to arrange interviews with "top-tier" candidates like Sen. Hillary Rodham Clinton (D) of New York or former New York City Mayor Rudolph Giuliani (R), it is clear that the most effective means for the politicians to gain momentum and support will be through the new and future Web 2.0 innovations.

So what is in it for me? Social networks allow us to express our concerns and interests to millions. Politicians are learning that the Internet fad is not a fad; it is a way of life. In September of 2006, Tom Gerace, founder and chief executive officer of Gather.com (which he billed as MySpace for grown-ups) identified the trend:

Politicians who ignore the impact of blogs and other social-networking sites will miss a huge number of potential voters. MySpace, which boasts 108 million profiles created by members, already reaches more people each day than CNN.com or NYTimes.com (as cited in Gross, 2006).

"Smart politicians will harness the power of social-networking sites, especially the ability to run videos within them. Politicians are just beginning to tap into the potential of social-networking sites," said Jeff Berman, Senior Vice President for Public Affairs at MySpace (as cited in Gross, 2006).

Social networks are one of the best ways to get your message out there. Just as email diminished the importance of the telephone, social networks are diminishing the importance of email. Certainly, there will be a continual need for it, but we are becoming less and less dependent on the "old" technology as the "new" technology emerges.

"You can be putting a message out there in far more powerful ways than just e-mailing or on your own website... Instead of pressing 'send' to half a million people today, it's activating a message that will be active for days thereafter," said Thomas Gensemer, Managing Director of Blue State Digital, said (Allison, 2007).

The most important thing to remember about social networks is that to use them effectively, **you must maintain the relationships you create**.

References

Allison, K. (2007, August 7). Battle for blogosphere ballot box heats up. *Financial Times*. Retrieved October 5, 2007, from http://www.ft.com/cms/s/0/d1f37eb2-450e-11dc-82f5-0000779fd2ac.html

Dickert, S. (2006, August 12). Will Social Networks Change Politics? *Political Gastronomica*. Retrieved October 5, 2007, from www.politicalgastronomica.com/archives/2006/08/will_social_net.html http://tinyurl.com/2htjtj

Feldmann, L. (2007, May 16). Web 2.0 meets Campaign 2008. *Christian Science Monitor*. Retrieved October 5, 2007 from http://www.csmonitor.com/2007/0516/p01s02-uspo.html

Gross, G. (2006, September 15). *Social networking sites: The next big thing in politics*. Retrieved October 5, 2007, from www.infoworld.com/article/06/09/15/HNsocialnetworkpolitics_1.html http://tinyurl.com/2lpmbx

Hindo, B. (2004, March 4). Meet John Kerry — on Friendster. *News Analysis – Business Week*. Retrieved October 5, 2007, from www.businessweek.com/bwdaily/dnflash/mar2004/nf2004034_6454 _db038.htm http://tinyurl.com/3arcu

Kotecki, J. (2007, April 26). *Congressman Ron Paul Visits My Dorm Room*. Retrieved October 7, 2007, from http://www.youtube.com/watch?v=nQi7PaYKqTU

Meetups in the News! (2006). *Newsweek covers on the affect of "social networks" on politics*. Retrieved October 5, 2007, from http://press.meetup.com/watch/archives/001523.html

Schmidt, T. S. (2006, September 6). *Inside the Backlash Against Facebook*. Retrieved October 5, 2007, from http://www.time.com/time/nation/article/0,8599,1532225,00.html

18 The Human Factors

Jay T. Deragon

If you review the history of human behavior, you will find both the roots that drive our behavior and the knowledge that changed it.

The roots start with the story of Adam and Eve, who were given all knowledge as long as they did not "take" the fruit from the Tree of Knowledge. Notice the emphasis of "take." From that time on, man was led to believe that taking was better than giving while battling the internal desires to give. As the world grew, and while different cultures migrated to communities then to tribes and then to countries, the essence of the mindset was driven by taking, while battling with those who said giving is better. People created and grew profit from their efforts, and business models were formed. Commerce began to spread, as did different cultures, religions, economies, and kingdoms.

Fast forward. The industrial era emerged, under the model of mass production for mass consumption, and the barons of industry were born. The barons became wealthy, and their businesses were about creating more results for the few and more consumable goods for the many. The law of decreasing returns showed that the yield rate, after a certain point, failed to increase in proportion to additional outlays of capital or investments of time and labor. It is the tendency for an application of effort or skill toward a particular project or goal to decline in effectiveness after a certain level of result has been achieved. In effect, it is the "glass ceiling" that dictates that no matter how hard a person works, only a certain amount of achievement can be reached.

During the late 18th and 19th centuries, the rich got richer while the working-class struggled to make ends meet. The apex of this era fell during the stock market crash. The "takers" took more and more while the "givers" went broke. In the industrial economy, success was self-limiting; it obeyed the law of decreasing returns (Kelly, 1998).

Enter world wars led by those who wanted to rule the world through the practice of taking by force. Millions have died because leaders wanted to "take" to support their beliefs of a new world.

Enter the era of technological explosion and information. Technology gave people and organizations tools with which to communicate and assimilate vast amounts of information. People began communicating faster and sharing more than was ever possible in the past. This explosive growth of information chartered the grounds for the knowledge era and has done so at speeds never before contemplated or comprehended. Technology accelerates the speed of change by enabling new knowledge, which creates new technology and subsequently, new human behavior.

New paradigms continue to be created more quickly than most humans have opportunities to acclimate. However, old paradigms remain, still heavily influenced with the "take" mentality—*what can I get from this or, what can I sell using this?* It is understandable when you look at history, our minds have been trained to think in the take mode while our hearts strive to give, and the battle continues.

Enter online social networking, which facilitates an old truism: Relationships drive everything. The younger generation migrates to this phenomenon in masses. Most will tell you they have better relationships online than offline. Considering that they are beginning to appreciate the model of social networks—relationships—taught to them through value shifts in society, one could understand how they may obtain

                                    Chapter 18: The Human Factors

perceived value and identity through on-line social networks versus at home or at school. However, the young again are teaching the old about opportunities to create a new world that satisfies the heart.

As the younger generation has discovered the benefits of on-line social networks, so the business community is beginning to follow suit. Intellectual property scholars note that many of the business markets straddle both the online and traditional world (Okediji, 2003). There appears to be a tendency to see these two locations as simply points along a continuum with certain aspects of business occurring online and others aspects occurring offline (Okediji, 2003). In The Relationship Economy, there will be no discernible difference between the two types of relationships.

With the likelihood of finding an identical match to yourself, unless you are a twin, being one of roughly 6 billion, it is undeniable that we all bring uniqueness to the table of networks to which we belong. Our life experiences shape us—intellectually, physically, emotionally and spiritually; this is what differentiates us from each other. Collectively our elements represent the gifts, abilities, and purpose we have, including both the good and bad, which we ultimately share with others through exchanges and future experiences.

Enter adult social networking. People spend time and money connecting with others online, but few are actually making any substantial money doing so. People share, help, express and participate with people they have never met but feel a kinship with based on communications. So, what causes these changes in human nature?

When we enter the virtual world, we do so with the history and experience in human relations of our physical world. With whom and with what we associate tends to follow the form of our physical world thus creating "our technological DNA of affinities." Our personality will affect how and where we use our gifts and abilities within virtual communities. For instance, two people may have similar intellectual knowledge and experiences, but if one is introverted and the other is extroverted, that intellectual knowledge will be expressed differently.

The more we participate within virtual worlds the more pronounced our technological DNA and virtual personalities become. Like stained glass, our different personalities reflect different shades of light within virtual communities. Our virtual life takes on different shapes as we begin to express ourselves to others individually and collectively through the groups in which we participate. In the same way our physical life is shaped by our physical world experiences of the past, our virtual life also takes shape based on the groups to which we belong and to whom we are connected. In determining our shape within the virtual world, one should consider what they desire for experiences in the future.

The Relationship Economy starts with changing the mindset of the masses, already happening through natural chaos. The mindsets we develop fulfill the heart's desire to give, and to realize doing so can be facilitated exponentially using technology. Our identities become anew – fulfilled with purpose based on our individual gifts, the richness of our relationships, and how many others we can reach by sharing our gifts.

The Relationship Economy is already gathering steam and amassing adopters who, without much of a tangible definition, are following their hearts and wondering why this feels so good. Kevin Kelly (1998), note-

          Chapter 18: The Human Factors

worthy author, said, "In a poetic sense, the prime goal of the new economy is to undo—company by company, industry by industry—the industrial economy" and we would add: individual by individual down to the essence of our being.

The Relationship Economy is not something one organization creates. Rather, it is the natural migration of human nature in mass looking for identity and fulfillment. Ironically, technology has enabled us to fulfill the very nature that resides in all of us, but has been heavily influenced by the history of traditional thinking, the paradigm of our minds where we have been taught to take rather than give.

Kelly (1998) stated, "Communication—which in the end is what digital technology and media are all about—is not just a sector of the economy. Communication is the economy."

In the world of plentiful networking opportunities, our struggle is not for finding connections but for finding meaning. As shown by the rise in volunteer work worldwide, people generally want to do things to help other people. It appears that altruism will play a significant role in the future, and that, ultimately, people are not focused on what they can get *from* others but what they can contribute to the lives of others. Individuals draw strength from quality, interdependent relationships, and often seek higher goals, such as a sense of belonging and identify a purpose in their lives (Sørensen, 2006).

Adults, in particular, have to overcome the restraints from their experiences in order to enjoy and satisfy a need for meaning. Because of individual experiences, many have not regained their focus to enjoy quality relationships, and thus satisfy their need for meaning. This lack of focus may have resulted from being hurt due to broken relationships, divorce, employment conflicts, family stress, and so on.

One of the main problems in understanding social networking is that some may assume that people behave utterly selfishly, which is untrue, because in many virtual communities people are being helped, encouraged, and fulfilled every day. Even the terminology used in the old economy may have been detrimental to the relationships themselves. Companies in the old economy prided themselves on "managing" relationships—treating people as "human capital" or "human assets" (Rayport and Jaworski, 2003). However, mechanistic production and rapacious consumption cannot contribute to a fulfilling life, much less substitute for one. Treating people as "human resources"—as tools for making money—is resulting in widespread stress, depression, and meaninglessness among both rich and poor in the so-called "developed" countries.

Some individuals seek only to "get" rather than "give" in the virtual world, and they approach a virtual community with the same view as they have with communities in the physical world. However, in many communities, altruism thrives because the people in the community help each other. Subsequently, the help each community member gives to others meets the very need for significance and esteem.

The "get" versus "give" mindset has affected the way business is conducted, as well. In The Relationship Economy, there are subtle and important differences from the traditional economy that influence the ways consumers and businesses behave (Wood, 2000). Some businesses understand the changes; they are focusing more on the existing or potential relationships that affect them, and many consumers are responding by frequenting those businesses (Wood, 2000).

To be successful in the virtual world one must go back to the basics of human composition and understand that giving is more satisfying than taking. It is imperative to have faith in the truism "give and it shall be given," or the approach to social networking will be with a jaded mind and heart, failing to comprehend and tap into the power of human nature accelerated by technology.

In The Relationship Economy, new terms are likely to appear, both to describe the business relationships between companies and those between companies and consumers. The traditional business model caused businesses to form and nurture long-term relationships with each other (Rayport and Jaworski, 2003)—the model in The Relationship Economy will force them to form and nurture long-term relationships with everyone.

References

Kelly, K. (1998). *New Rules for the New Economy.* Retrieved September 1, 2007, from http://www.kk.org/newrules

Okediji, R. L. (2003). *Development in the Information Age: Issues in the Regulation of Intellectual Property Rights, Computer Software and Electronic Commerce* (Draft). Retrieved October 10, 2007, from www.iprsonline.org/unctadictsd/docs/Okediji_ECommerce.Dec03.pdf http://tinyurl.com/24ff5a

Rayport, J. F. and Jaworski, B. J. (2003). *Introduction to E-Commerce* (2nd ed.). New York: McGraw-Hill.

Sørensen, K. (2006). *Maslow's hierarchy of needs and subpersonality work.* Retrieved October 17, 2007, from http://two.not2.org/psychosynthesis/articles/maslow.htm

Wood, I. M. (2000). *The Bucks $tart Here: How Great Digital Companies Create Lasting Business Value.* Milford, CT: Capstone.

Carter F. Smith

Learning is not compulsory... neither is survival.
— W. Edwards Deming (1900 - 1993)

Terabytes of information are exchanged between hundreds of millions of individuals globally. From these conversations, we are individually and collectively inspired to learn of a new world, fueled by a Relationship Economy where the overriding factor of value appears to be our ability to learn. Learning is a lifelong process. Even those who are leaders in their organization must learn on a regular basis. In *The Adult Learner,* Knowles, Holton, and Swanson (2005) identified the strong link between leading and learning. Knowles is known as the "father" of modern andragogy. Andragogy is the "art and science of leading adults." Leaders must be both proficient in learning and proficient in leading others through their own personal learning process.

The overwhelming pace at which change occurs, relationships are built, and business is done appears to serve as a catalyst for both leadership and learning. Leadership is needed to maintain order and guide individuals and organizations through previously uncharted territory as they move through often-strange surroundings with the speed provided (and required) by Internet time. The learning zone in these times is a synthesis of new ideas and excitement, often mixed with some confusion. It may feel uncomfortable, especially for the consummate professional, but that is precisely how it is supposed to be.

The optimal zone in which adults learn is referred to as *disjuncture*—when time seems to stop. . . when our biographical repertoire is no longer sufficient to cope automatically with our situation. . . where we have a tension with our environment (Jarvis, 2006). Without entering this zone, we are simply stacking up our experiences on top of things to which we can relate. This action often leads to an unnecessary compromise, where we settle for what is readily available to us, rather than what is actually the best fit. With disjuncture, we are forced to build a completely new structure of learning. While in the disjuncture zone, though we usually will experience discomfort, we are ultimately able to establish a strong foundation for *real* learning.

Many people equate learning with an educational institution. They may have a very shallow definition of learning, limiting it to various educational institutions and for a select few of the population. While these institutions serve a valuable purpose for the development of the individual, it is not their sole purpose. It is at these places, for the most part, where we interact with different people, develop interpersonal relationships, and acquire a working knowledge of the real world.

Chapter 19: The Learning Factors

Today's students use modern technology in their everyday activities, and the way they communicate *now* is likely to influence how they communicate in the future as they enter the workforce in numbers that will cause us to rethink how things are done. Most of today's college students have an online presence and regularly communicate online in some form (Oblinger & Oblinger, 2005; Sreebny, 2007). Today's social networking sites are often the medium used to establish this online presence, and they are increasingly attracting return visits on a regular basis. On the first day of college, 85 percent of college students have a Facebook account; by the end of the first semester, and due to various internal or external influences, 94 percent of college students have a Facebook account (Sreebny, 2007).

Students need these interactive environments to help them grasp the complicated and controversial content inherent in the material they are learning, both in the classroom and in their new life away from the home of their parents. They will also use these environments as they enter the professional community and engage in collaborative teamwork, project management, and shortened deadlines. If they will be expected to survive in the pre-defined business world, they will need to understand how these environments can be used for their benefit, and the rest of us will need to help them learn.

Most of our learning, especially in higher education, comes from a secondary experience (Jarvis, 2006). With established social networks, we are able to build connections with many others who have experiences that are vastly different from our own. By engaging with them in a mutual and mutually beneficial learning experience, we are able to collectively engage in the learning process and increase our potential for learning. At the same time, we are strengthening our trusted connections with others as we share our experiences with them. These relationships will continue long past the handing out of diplomas and the tossing of tasseled headwear.

This phenomenon has not escaped the attention of researchers, both in academia and in the business community. Many in higher education are using, or to some extent evaluating the use of, contemporary social networking technology such as MySpace or Facebook (Carnevale, 2006). Though the reasons for such exploration are varied, the essence appears to be that learning always occurs in a social context (Jarvis, 2006).

By capitalizing on the use of social networks while students attend college, faculty and other school leaders can not only strengthen the learning foundation for students, but can also maintain contact with students as they go out into the community following graduation. College administrators can strategically use social networks to stay in contact with graduates in hopes of garnering a loyal cadre of alumni.

For students, taking part in social networks while in college offers benefits for the future. Networking can be a means of establishing connections within the community they will enter upon graduation. As alumni, they can show loyalty to their alma mater by offering employment to future graduates, support to athletic organizations, and financial contribution to the institution.

Neither the concept of learning nor the rapid growth in usage of social networking technology is limited to learning institutions. Learning is a lifelong journey with wondrous surprises awaiting the journeyman. Learning is a constantly evolving organism that knows no limits and is constantly developing the human mind into new ways of thinking, acting, doing, and living. Learning is the root of past discoveries and civilizations, the backbone of present ones and the catalyst of future ones. It is essentially what separates us from animals, and is exceedingly imperative in developing a closer, more intimate relationship with the Creator of the universe. Without it, humanity would be virtually non-existent.

The common dictionary meaning for learning is "knowledge acquired by study." By studying certain subjects found in books and magazines, such as mathematics or science, one can gather a concrete knowledge of the subject matter. By studying people, events and places around one, one can gather a general understanding of how they operate. By taking the time to study oneself, one can gather a healthy, thorough, legitimate knowledge of oneself and how to improve. There is no doubt that learning is essential for the human being to survive and thrive.

The purpose of learning is to enhance and develop the human mind, and to develop, nurture, and enhance civilization. The purpose is to obtain learning and to share learning so that everybody can benefit, since everyone has to live in this world.

          Chapter 19: The Learning Factors

Conclusion

There is much to learn about the emergence of our virtual world. Numerous factors are inter-related and the convergence of global conversations is creating the abundance of information, which in turn is defining new knowledge that requires learning like never before in our history.

The operators, the media, and the technological providers—for their own purposes aimed primarily at economic gains—are maximizing their understanding of the knowledge of the power and the use of social networks. When the majority of individuals participating within the medium of social networks begin to learn beyond "how to use" the medium and move to the strategic use of "purpose driven business and personal objectives," we will see a rapid shift of power and focus.

The Relationship Economy will emerge faster than the medium that enabled its emergence as individuals learn how to leverage their power and their networks. The Relationship Economy will be born out of the simplicity of collective purpose and understanding. Simplicity is a tipping point when collective experiences and information emerges as well defined knowledge and pathways shared with the masses. We hope to facilitate the emergence by providing the research, the tools, and clarity to the pathways of success.

References

Carnevale, D. (2006). E-Mail is for Old People. *The Chronicle of Higher Education,* 53(7), A.27.

Jarvis, P. (2006). *Towards a Comprehensive Theory of Human Learning.* New York: Routledge.

Knowles, M. S., Holton, E. F. II, and Swanson, R. A. (2005). *The Adult Learner.* (6th Ed.). Burlington, MA: Elsevier.

Oblinger, D.G. and Oblinger, J. L. (2005). Is It Age or IT: First Steps Toward Understanding the Net Generation. In D.G. Oblinger and J. L. Oblinger (Eds.), *Educating the Net Generation* (pp. 12-31). Boulder, CO: EDUCAUSE. Retrieved January 31, 2008, from http://www.educause.edu/content.asp?page_id=6058&bhcp=1

Sreebny, O. (2007). *Digital rendezvous: Social software in higher education.* EDUCAUSE Center for Applied Research, 2007(2). Retrieved January 31, 2008, from www.connect.educause.edu/ Library/ ECAR/DigitalRendezvousSocialSo/40158 http://tinyurl.com/2hewbv

20 The Industry Factors

Carter F. Smith

Many of the factors we have identified and discussed are viewed in the context of traditional business organizations. This chapter will examine some of the challenges faced in a variety of industries when considering the changes brought about by the use of social networking and other Relationship Economy catalysts.

Whatis.com defines social networking as "the practice of expanding the number of one's business and/or social contacts by making connections through individuals" (Social Networking, 2007). They note that the "unparalleled potential of the Internet" serves as a major catalyst, and that social networking sites serve to "help people make contacts that would be good for them to know, but that they would be unlikely to have met otherwise" (Social Networking, 2007).

Social networking has been increasingly accepted in traditional businesses, but not so in others. The changes brought about by The Relationship Economy will be examined with the lenses of three industries: Government (Law Enforcement), Services, and Manufacturing, which have not been quick adopters.

pina iannuzzi, 2007

Law Enforcement

Providing law enforcement services to the community involves a unique mixture of talents and techniques. There are many service functions provided by law enforcement organizations, and a variety of specialty services provided by its members. Consequently, Law Enforcement is one of the government industries that will be drastically affected by the changes brought about in The Relationship Economy.

Many traditional businesses have increased their consideration of virtual workforces in response to a variety of precursors to The Relationship Economy. There may initially appear to be limited application for this model in traditional law enforcement operations. However, if we stand on top of the box and reexamine the application, we may find this model useful. If computer companies can outsource their customer service to another country, it seems feasible that non-emergency calls for law enforcement service could be sent to an appropriately outfitted home office. With voice technology currently able to record and store conversations virtually (see the developments of Google's Grand Central as an example), could this change how we look at police dispatch?

Social networking, as we have mentioned elsewhere, requires us to transform our thinking. We are not suggesting a radical implementation of a set of inflexible technologies. The suggestion is to use more of an a-la-carte approach to see how specific technology implementation would benefit certain operations. If law enforcement organizations intend to be effective in the new economy, they will have to reevaluate their business models on a regular basis.

One example of an opportunity to reexamine existing business practices and apply new technology would be the ever-present challenge in law enforcement intelligence known as "connecting the dots." This challenge is experienced when communication between related groups or teams (even in the same department) breaks down to the point that the job of intelligence collection, analysis, and dissemination cannot be accomplished easily, consistently, effectively, or in a timely manner. This miscommunication or lack of communication often occurs when a representative from one team chooses not to contact another because there was no pre-established trust relationship. Pre-established social and professional networks—whether augmented by technology or not—will facilitate this communication and the process where the dots can be connected.

To an extent, law enforcement organizations can benefit from the work tempo increase enabled by the technology. Officers on the street presently serve the public in a variety of roles, many of which are time consuming, and technology that streamlines such work would be beneficial.

There is significant public strategic value of a law enforcement community built around a knowledge sharing culture, where a large law enforcement network with weak internal personal ties is transformed into a network where many individuals find commonalities and form personal relationships. Social networking is beneficial to law enforcement, the public, and criminals alike.

Many organizations have examined the replacement of email by inter-intra-agency use of wikis. Law enforcement organizations could become even more effective if all their policies and procedures were maintained in a central location—such as a virtual bulletin board that could be edited by a select number of leaders, with an update notice to email, internal mail, or mobile phone text message, to notify the user of the changes on an immediate basis.

We should consider adding our local police officer or precinct to our contacts or friends list. These individuals and organizations exist already in our community network, and possibly our social network of friends. Imagine community policing enhanced by a display of trusted connections, personal photos, or random thoughts. Customers who aggregate and form interest groups will be able to influence the private sector through comments and postings and interactions. Citizens who form virtual communities could share information within that community. Professional use is the number one reason many join an online community, and sometimes it overlaps social use.

If law enforcement took advantage of existing technology, we envision the process of a phone call to the police station being replaced by a posting on the virtual wall of the police station's Web site. If we are members of a variety of groups that include our neighborhood, volunteer watch patrols, perhaps even the Tuesday-Thursday carpool, some of our regular communications are likely made via text message from our mobile computing devices in the new economy.

A concerned group of individuals or citizens will impact government agencies of all kinds. The concept of customer service in government will be a reality in The Relationship Economy.

A convenience-sampling search for "law enforcement" on the worldwide social networking sites Facebook, MySpace, and LinkedIn was conducted, which produced interesting results.

The Facebook account yielded over 500 profiles for individuals listing their profession as "law enforcement." It should be noted that Facebook limits the results to 500, does not limit the search to profession, and does not report higher numbers. A follow-up search limiting

     Chapter 20: The Industry Factors

the results to "Job Title: police" was conducted, also yielding 500 results. A search for law enforcement yielded only six. This search was conducted with 316 friends on the profile.

A general search for "Law Enforcement" on the MySpace account yielded 93,400, but contained links to groups, postings, and other non-profile data. By limiting the search to "general interests," a return of 361 profiles was found. A general search for "Police" yielded 5,000 results. These searches were conducted with 69 Friends on the profile.

The LinkedIn account yielded over 500 user profiles for individuals listing their profession as "law enforcement." It should be noted that LinkedIn also limits the results to 500, and does not report higher numbers. This search was conducted with 186 contacts on the profile.

The purpose of these searches was to ensure there were a sufficient number of those engaged in the law enforcement profession with some form of social (professional) networking presence. These sites could be useful to those engaged in law enforcement activity for making and maintaining contact for social and professional purposes. Further, re-cruiting for jobs occurs on these sites, and it is anticipated that services such as real-time collaborative conferencing including audio, video, and text will be found invaluable in the law enforcement field. As the public sector follows the private sector, we can expect to see numerous areas of specialty communities develop, which are comprised of those involved in the investigation of drug crimes, gangs, and even traffic offenses, for example.

For those in the law enforcement field, online communications poses major concerns regarding privacy. Law enforcement officials inherently need to establish a trust relationship in order to communicate effective-ly face-to-face with criminals, witnesses, etc. How much will that change in a digital encounter?

Additionally, software downloads (designed to enhance user experi-ence) may be prohibited by the organization's technology department. The need to install even a minimally intrusive piece of software might frustrate the user enough to cause him or her to avoid the connection that would benefit them the most. The potential solution for this might be a Web-based third party aggregator service that would be designed to simplify the use and maintenance of multiple profiles, and can collect and distribute updates in both push and pull form without requiring the installation of additional software.

As with any other industry, initial apprehension from the organization's leadership is expected. Security will be addressed, and prohibitive measures against the counterproductive use of the technology will be taken. There may also be challenges with encouraging open communication and dialog between co-workers. These challenges come in demonstrating the value of this technology and then teaching people how to use the basic tools of the information age, which is not peculiar to law enforcement, but will add an additional complexity for the police officer on the street, as an example.

There should not be a lock-step application. Individuals will naturally fill roles within the various segments of their communities, often taking what was learned in one to apply in another. There will be some who ask questions. Others will answer. Some will post blogs, and others will comment on them. In the end, it is all classified as communication.

Services

According to the United States Census Bureau, the services industries account for 55 percent of economic activity in the U.S. The services industry as referred to by the Census Bureau includes consultants, trainers, financial advisers, communications providers, publishing, an assortment of technology designers, and the sales forces and support personnel within and peripheral to those industries. The services affected by the early stages of The Relationship Economy can be limited only by the vision of those providing such services.

Increasing numbers of healthcare, scientific, and other professionals are not limited by the need for ongoing face-to-face contact, and appear to be prepared for engagement in the new economy. In addition, the nature of providing services requires the ability to adapt to changing needs; thus for those in the services industry, the use of social networking technology is not as daunting as it can be for other industries. Because technology can be a boost to productivity and desired outcomes, the use of technological tools is on the rise in the services sector.

The services industry appears well positioned to benefit from the increased acceptance of the virtual workforce. Many service providers are on the cutting edge of such trends and easily accept the need to transform their thinking and build long-distance relationships based on trust. This industry grasps the strategic value of "digging your well before you are thirsty," and naturally makes and strengthens connections in order to learn about the potential synergy they have with others in order to develop new clientele.

The usual strategy of the services industry is to amass a collection of business cards (or contacts), often resulting in a large network of weak ties. The strength of social networking provides options that allow for strengthening some of those ties. This group naturally connects with new people who have similar interests and instinctively looks for common ground on which to develop their relationships. The services have already recognized that aggregate groups of customers can influence prices and offerings, and they are likely to adapt to those demands as easily in digitally based relationships as they have in the face-to-face model.

Service organizations and businesses engaged in The Relationship Economy will realize increased productivity. Their increased connectivity and mobility will require flexible and responsive systems in time management and customer relationship management. Communications in The Relationship Economy including real-time collaborative conferencing, using audio, video and text, will provide a venue in which much of the *personal touch* in services can be (virtually) felt.

Those providing services seem to have a unique place when it comes to addressing what is identified as the "Digital Divide." The Digital Divide refers to the gap that exists between the "Haves" and "Have-Nots" regarding access to technology. Those businesses that have "service to consumer" services will have to bridge this gap in order to provide services to a select number of their potential customer base. For example, those providers of geriatric health care may find that many of their clients may not have access to or the mental or physical capability to use technology. It is expected that many companies will offer tutorials to teach clientele who have access how to use the technology necessary to exchange information that supports the required services.

The May 2007 survey conducted by the Institute for Corporate Productivity noted that of those who use social networking technologies, 55 percent use them to share best practices and answer questions (Vickers, 2007). Of those surveyed, 47 percent use their networks to connect with potential clients and showcase their skills, while 55 percent do so to share best practices with colleagues, and 49 percent use them to get answers to issues they are currently facing (Vickers, 2007). These are all indicative of a strong foundational use of consulting (which emphasizes best practices) and other services, and while the percentages are already relatively high, they are expected to continue their growth.

Those who provide training for a living recognize that online learning opportunities add many new possibilities to their repertoire. Most times, online education and training do not require face-to-face encounters. However, some educational institutions chose to require an on-site experience. Often, an introductory training session can precede a more intense face-to-face training, allowing the attendees to

     Chapter 20: The Industry Factors

establish a comfort level with the material and the trainer. In the same way, follow-up on-line sessions can wrap-up the study, and provide continued dialog that reinforce the learning process.

The banking industry has asserted itself as a powerful online presence for some time. As the client base becomes increasingly comfortable with technology-based communication, transactions that started with an office meeting and culminated with a mailing or facsimile transmission can be completed in far less time with a Web site visit, or even a simple mobile phone text message.

The services industry is expected to continue to lead the way in The Relationship Economy, fueled by the needs of its clients and the opportunities provided by technology improvements. Each of the areas in this industry can expect to change from the way in which they conduct business as they adopt new technologies.

Manufacturing

All facets of the manufacturing industry are affected by The Relationship Economy. The evolution of The Relationship Economy will affect operations and physical plants across international borders. The manufacturing sector is expected to have the biggest potential for change of those examined here because it affects international commerce as well as individual consumption. Change will be required and rewarded in this industry, and opportunities for growth will abound.

The trade of manufacturers is raw material and the process that transforms it. Prices are set, markets are stabilized, and business is conducted—often with the same suppliers. Once a relationship is developed, repeat business between the same suppliers and buyers stabilizes and strengthens it.

With the exception of a few administrative functions, the use of a virtual workforce for many manufacturing functions is not possible. The change to the manufacturing model will be shifted if most processes are performed virtually. In addition, if the industry's actual manufacturing component, including quality control over production, moves outsides a particular country, it will affect the real estate property of the original country. The evolution of The Relationship Economy will effect operations and physical plants across international borders.

As those in the manufacturing sector transform their thinking, they may do well to choose wisely when looking for the best place for a new facility. The Relationship Economy appears poised to affect the way manufacturers conduct recruiting, determine output, and market what they produce. These changes will require a workforce comprised of individuals who can understand the significance of such a rapidly changing paradigm. Those who ignore the potential for change are likely to be engulfed by it.

The effect of The Relationship Economy on manufacturing will be increased productivity and efficiency. Consumers will collectively demand that products are of superior quality, that they are of sufficient amount and variety, and that they be available without unnecessary delay. Manufacturers will be required to do more than listen—they will need to ask us what we want —and deliver it using both production and social media processes.

     Chapter 20: The Industry Factors

The manufacturing sector may have the highest number of employees experiencing the Digital Divide—the gap between the "haves" and "have-nots" regarding access to technology because many of their employees have no current need to use social media in order to produce products. It may serve the industry well if it provides opportunities to train employees on the use of basic technology. This may involve allowing access to public social networking sites on company time, or designing in-house networking sites.

Further, manufacturers in The Relationship Economy will need to find effective ways to evoke positive experiences outside of traditional marketing channels. Relationship building with the end-users through the medium of social networking will be the starting point. Company employees represent the company even when they do not intend to do so. In The Relationship Economy, policies for interaction outside the company, though likely to be considered intrusive, should be provided for in those situations where employees have provided a visible connection to the company in their profiles.

Manufacturers will have to take steps to caution against counter productivity for those engaged in communicating—both those on the company's time and those working on the company's behalf. It will have to address the synergy between physical production requirements and those processes that can be enhanced through employing social media technologies. In addition, it will have to address the employees' expectations that they have access to social media during business hours and the companies' interests on social media sites, which will have an impact on The Relationship Economy.

References

Social Networking. Retrieved October 16, 2007, from
   http://whatis.techtarget.com/definition/0,,sid9_gci942884,00.html
   http://tinyurl.com/3yuuro

Vickers, M. (2007, June 8). Does Social Networking Boost
   Productivity?, American Management Association.
   Retrieved January 31, 2008, from
   http://www.amanet.org/performance-profits/editorial.cfm?Ed=549

21 | The Planning Factors

Jay T. Deragon

"The Planning Factors" are just that: factors that must be considered in planning one's future actions. They consist of examining the entire system of The Relationship Economy, and ensuring that all the factors are considered for one's future social networking. One method of context analysis, factor analysis, also known as environmental scanning, is a method to analyze the environment, including personal factors and the macro environment, in which a business operates (Context analysis, 2007).

This is an important aspect of a strategic planning process as organizations and individuals enter the social networking space. Because the factors of The Relationship Economy are highly dynamic and ever changing, the process of factor analysis must be a continual process rather than a single "event" that occurs in the life of a business.

Time Factors	Influence Factors	Political Factors
Knowledge Factors	Media Factors	Cultural Factors
Relationship Factors	Gender Factors	Human Factors
Networked Factors	Age Factors	Learning Factors
Technology Factors	Individual Factors	Industry Factors
Economic Factors	Relationship Capital Factors	Planning Factors
Systemic Factors	Us Factors	Future Factors

Jay Deragon : www.linktoyourworld.com

An older method of context analysis, called SWOT (Strengths, Weaknesses, Opportunities, and Threats) analysis, allows a business to gain an insight into those four categories posed by the market within which it operates (Context analysis, 2007). In factor analysis, we are more inclined to examine not only the market in which we are operating, but also the shared and even the peripheral environments between the primary market and related markets. This complex examination requires a "vision" that is referred to as *systemic*, or *systems thinking* (Senge, 2006). *Systems thinking* describes the process of understanding the entire system by contemplating the whole, not simply the individual parts—the fifth dimension (Senge, 2006). Senge's focus on systems thinking encourages us to take a step backward, to consider what may not appear directly in front of us, to attempt to understand how smaller events can change the larger collection of events.

While application of SWOT is appropriate in helping to determine whether social network(s) are or would be a value-add to your business, it does not apply to determination of which platform or platforms would be appropriate. This alteration in the process requires research and analysis of both current and future factors of this emerging space. The alteration also requires that SWOT analysis is considered in context to this dynamic environment.

Chapter 21: The Planning Factors

Research on the driving factors that influence the social networking market in light of current and future conditions shows many significant factors of influence. When evaluating initial factors, the use of an inter-relationship and affinity diagram enables us to sort through the collective meaning of the factors and then categorize them—effectively determining and ranking how the categories relate to and influence each other.

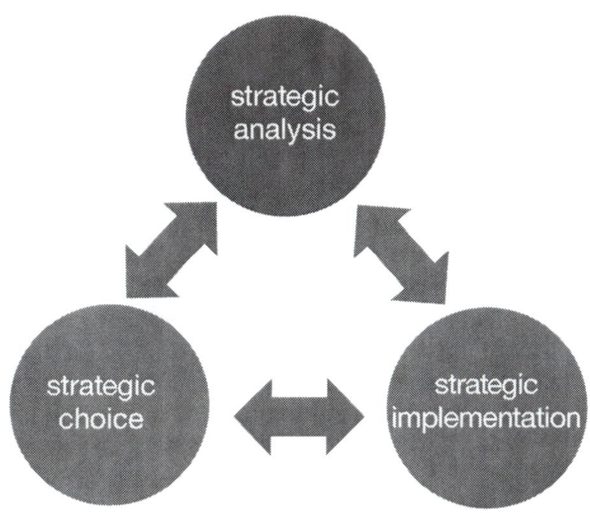

Jay Deragon : www.linktoyourworld.com

The relationship between the categories is defined by which category drives the others (most to least), with subsequent outcomes being out/in arrows. The category with the most "out" arrows has the greatest influence on the collective factor outcomes. This method of analysis is likely to produce different outcomes when applied by different individuals, organizations, or institutions in the context of their opportunities to leverage their network to meet their objectives within the emerging space of The Relationship Economy.

Each category may produce different results based on the question, "How can we leverage social networking mediums to our advantage?" That question establishes the direction of the above example by shaping the context for analysis. Subsequently, the outcomes of these exercises provide the roadmap for prioritization of initiatives, actions, or investments—all aimed at accomplishing the individual's or business's objectives.

While the research and reporting on the factors thus far identified continues, additional factors continue to emerge in this rapidly expanding area. Newly identified factors should be included in this analysis in the future by each segment of the market as it enters the social media space. The social networking space is dynamic, and therefore, considerations must be made to manage The Relationship Economy appropriately.

Anyone who is serious about capitalizing on the opportunities through social media must develop a plan that includes a system that reports on the changes that occur on a daily basis. One technique could be to alter the traditional balanced scorecard tool for ongoing assessment and feedback, which facilitates the establishment of monitoring systems. In addition, the process of planning can be easily changed to respond to market influences and technological developments. The balanced scorecard has been used to clarify and update budgets, identify and align strategic initiatives, and conduct periodic performance reviews to learn about and improve strategy (Balanced scorecard, 2007).

Convergence of devices, networks, networking platforms, multiple mediums, and content within the social computing space is the subject of interest. The execution of convergence is happening. Much of it is happening behind the scenes, but will not be for much longer. The combined convergence will result in significant disruption in numerous social computing models that have not even had time to mature.

Recently, we witnessed additional technology that enables individuals to connect their profile in social networks, their content, videos, and everything else across their computer, TVs and cell phone—seamlessly. In addition, we now have the ability to run live video conferencing directly from a personal profile.

The cover story of the September 2007 issue of *Business 2.0* was "The Next Disruptors." It focused on the potential grip that social networking technologies have on current business practices. The subtitle read, "Watch Out, GE, AT&T, United, Microsoft, and even Google. These 10 new companies are getting set to roll up markets." The subtitle provides us with a viewpoint as to how hot the market is for social networking content and providers.

The article provided this advice:

1. **Sell Ads:** Developers who launch applications on Facebook are generating income from advertising.

2. **Attract Sponsors:** Some developers are using sponsors to launch their applications.

3. **Sell Services:** Some creative firms are promoting services on Facebook through widgets and advertising media.

4. **Sell Products:** Facebook has established a marketplace for the sale of products, and soon the executives will be launching their own ecommerce engine to facilitate sales directly through Facebook applications.

Does this sound like The Relationship Economy? The next path of migration must be centered on the individual user's ability to create an economy of his or her own. When that happens, it will be the genesis of The Relationship Economy. This will enable millions of individuals to exchange value for economic gains. The pathway for individual gains will follow institutions, governments, and corporations creating their own marketplace of exchange within social networks. Ultimately, all this activity will roll downhill to individuals who are connecting, socializing, communicating, and buying and selling. The collective activity represents the emergence of The Relationship Economy—born in the virtual world and enabled by advanced technology. Our vision of the future will become reality.

What is certain is that change has been happening and *will continue to* happen at lightning speeds. This is not a space for the faint of heart; rather it is for the dynamic aggressors who can see the future and plan to be there before others arrive. Planning for disruption and being on the cutting edge are the initial steps necessary for defining future opportunities. Much needs to be considered and sorted out with clarity, and doing so requires a comprehensive approach while focusing on the factors that enable success.

Business Uses of Social Networks Today

Many of a particular advertising company's employees were spending a portion of their workday on a public access social network site. In response, the company leadership launched a network of their own, for employees only. Today, a little more than a third of the company's workers have signed up for their own pages where they can create profiles that outline their jobs, list the brands they admire, and describe their values (Workplace, 2007).

What the company chose to do was to focus inward instead of outward. The company decided to channel or guide the natural actions of its employee. It had the opportunity to find ways to help the employees market their company brand while engaging in social networking with other individuals who were not employees of that company.

Mainstream traditional companies also are looking at the fast-growing social network scene as a place to market their products, and many are adopting similar Web technology to create internal networks. It is an efficient way to mine for in-house expertise, discover new recruits, and share information within their own walls. However, establishing a corporate version of a social network has its own challenges, because companies have to build in safeguards to ensure compliance with requirements and protect privacy (Green, 2007).

Employees are pushing companies to recognize the impact of social networks. Corporate employees are building lists of contacts from among the more than 17 million professionals on LinkedIn. At Ernst and Young alone, 11,000 workers now have Facebook accounts (Workplace, 2007). By offering employees a social network, companies hope to obtain the benefit of leveraging the employee's skills and contacts, while also providing a collaborative environment that will cut out time that employees spend mailing documents and e-mailing comments (Workplace, 2007).

This volume of participants translates into a potential marketing opportunity of enormous proportions. It is particularly opportunistic for tech companies that sell networking products. Everyone from IBM to Microsoft to startups such as intro Net-works, Awareness Inc., and Jive Software are offering applications and services. One company, Select-Minds, has created social networks for 60 companies, including

Lockheed Martin and JPMorgan Chase (Green, 2007). Moreover, SharePoint, the Microsoft software that lets companies set up MySpace-like profiles, blogs, and collaborative Web sites (known as wikis within the confines of their firewalls), is one of the fastest-growing server products in the company's history (Green, 2007). "At first people were slow to adopt this; they were nervous. But now we're seeing a bunch of adoption," says Rob Curry, director of the Microsoft Office SharePoint Server software (Workplace, 2007). Both Microsoft and IBM are using their own offices as labs for their products.

These techniques are also gathering momentum in knowledge management. IBM introduced a platform called Lotus Connections that allows company employees to post detailed profiles of themselves, collaborate on projects, share bookmarks, and identify in-house expertise. Another company is testing the software to put inexperienced members of its customer-services team in touch with engineers that can assist them and their customers (Jardin, 2007). Software firms will probably start bundling social features of this kind into all sorts of business software (Jardin, 2007).

Example of Using the Planning Process for Corporate Benefit

Company A, a consulting firm specializing strategic development for many Fortune 500 companies, followed the planning process illustrated above and came away with a new plan of action.

After facilitating an analysis of their own SWOT in relation to this emerging space, they discovered the following:

1. They could leverage the social medium technology to increase value to existing clients.

2. They could leverage the medium to improve their position as thought leaders within the selected industry segments they serve.

3. They could build or transform existing practice units into experts in deploying strategic plans for others seeking to capture the opportunities presented by the medium of social networks.

4. They could use the medium to improve internal operational processes such as communications, coordination of task, and collaboration amongst dispersed resources.

5. They could leverage the medium for the purposes of creating market differential through development and deployment of proprietary technology that enhances the medium and social media efforts.

From these initial strategic opportunities, the company then rated which of the above would help drive the organizations overall financial objectives. They concluded that #1 should be the starting point, and decided to use this experience as a case study for their own clients and as a medium to communicate the value proposition of social computing and their own depth of knowledge.

Subsequently, the company appointed a small team to lead the process and report to the executive committee with specific execution-able tasks, timelines, and budgets, as well as expected returns. This initial team would later become the company's leading resource relative to the plan and the subject matter.

Six months after implementing the plan, the company was amazed at how receptive the market was to the newly introduced tools and the firm's expertise, which provided assistance to prospective firms that wanted to leverage their own objectives using the medium of social networks and related factors.

The race is on. Those who will win using the new medium and its related power are those that define the very factors driving their market, their customers, and their operations, as well as those who have finely-honed execution skills and respond to changes with lightening speed.

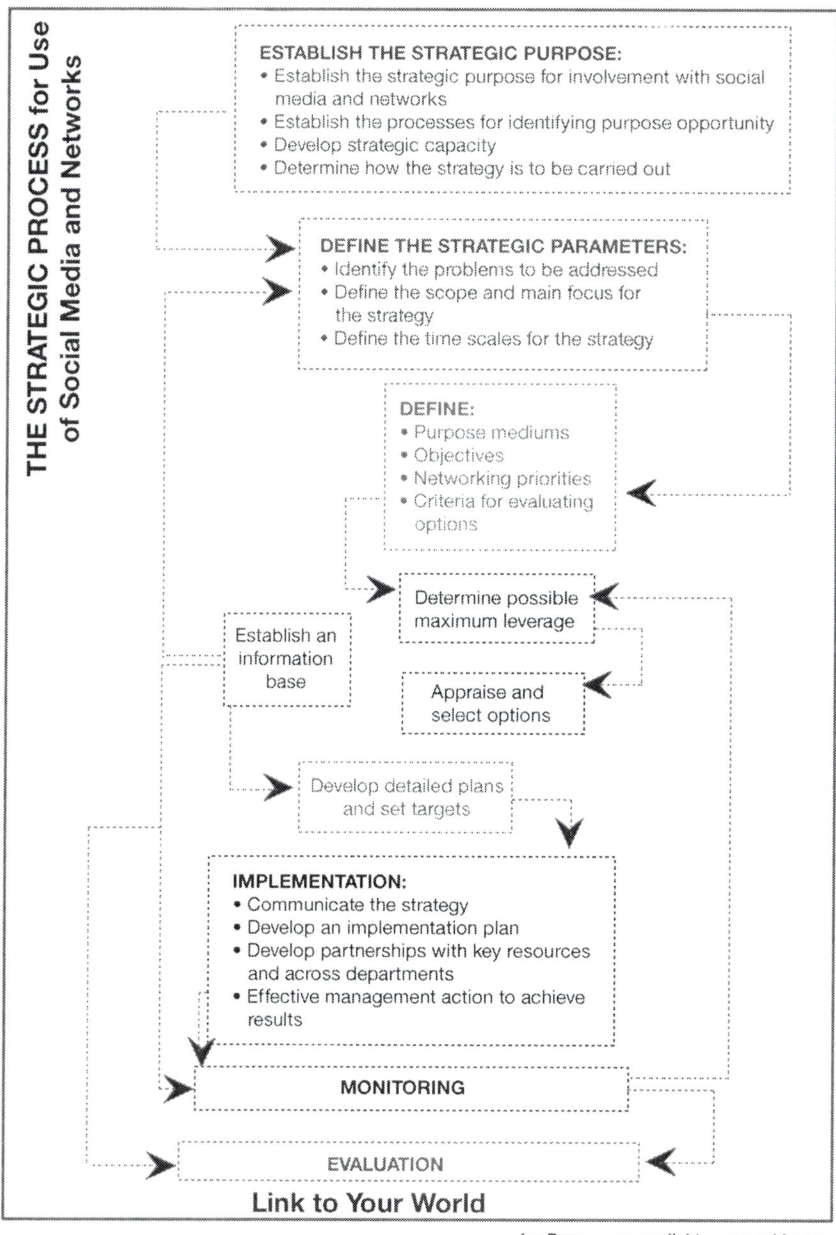

THE STRATEGIC PROCESS for Use of Social Media and Networks

ESTABLISH THE STRATEGIC PURPOSE:
• Establish the strategic purpose for involvement with social media and networks
• Establish the processes for identifying purpose opportunity
• Develop strategic capacity
• Determine how the strategy is to be carried out

DEFINE THE STRATEGIC PARAMETERS:
• Identify the problems to be addressed
• Define the scope and main focus for the strategy
• Define the time scales for the strategy

DEFINE:
• Purpose mediums
• Objectives
• Networking priorities
• Criteria for evaluating options

Determine possible maximum leverage

Establish an information base

Appraise and select options

Develop detailed plans and set targets

IMPLEMENTATION:
• Communicate the strategy
• Develop an implementation plan
• Develop partnerships with key resources and across departments
• Effective management action to achieve results

MONITORING

EVALUATION

Link to Your World

Jay Deragon : www.linktoyourworld.com

Note that this model begins with establishing a (strategic) purpose. The word "purpose" probably draws a nod—perhaps even a stifled yawn from many in business (Morgan, 2006). Few owners would admit to a commitment to a purpose and the long term that fades in and out. Yet purpose is not as pervasive and easy as it sounds. Purpose means that quality decisions are not situational. The advent of social networking mediums is creating a stir within the business community across all markets globally, but has business defined its purpose?

Given that a primary purpose of any business is to serve its customers efficiently and effectively with the value proposition that they offer, one must then consider the impending impact of social mediums on that purpose. However, will business leaders react and jump into social media without a clear purpose in mind?

Are social networks situational or do they represent strategic shifts of strategic importance?

Robert Young (2006) has written about social networks as a platform for self-expression, and noted how new media shifts the balance of control for production and distribution of content between corporations and consumers. He has also written about the strategic implications of these shifts and the business model challenges that face any player attempting to monetize social media.

There is another critical aspect of social networking, however, that will serve as the anchor component for social networks as they begin to enter their next stage of evolutionary development. This component is the communications layer embedded within social networks (Young, 2006).

It is equally important to realize that communications alone, especially a new form such as walls, does not necessarily act as the primary draw for new users (Young, 2006). For example, going back to the early days of consumer online services, email was not a very effective draw to acquire new users. This occurred primarily because most people had no idea what email was and how useful it could be. Therefore, other benefits, such as unique content, were emphasized to acquire new users. Yet, once users discovered the benefits of email, it became the common ubiquitous activity among the community. As a result, it is

Chapter 21: The Planning Factors

critical to understand that what attracts people initially is often not what keeps people on your network interested and vested in the long run... a dynamic that is a critical guide for strategic planning (2006).

While communications is a critical factor for every business, it is not the only factor to consider. As the business markets become more and more engaged with the medium of social networks, it is of critical importance that they define the "purpose" of their involvement. Once a clear purpose is defined, then, as our diagram illustrates, one can expect to map out effective strategies and actions to fulfill the stated purpose.

Strategies followed by actions can be measured to verify intent and to determine whether those actions are fulfilling stated purposes. Situational reactions to the growth of the social media implementation strategies will only end in wasted time, energy, and expenses.

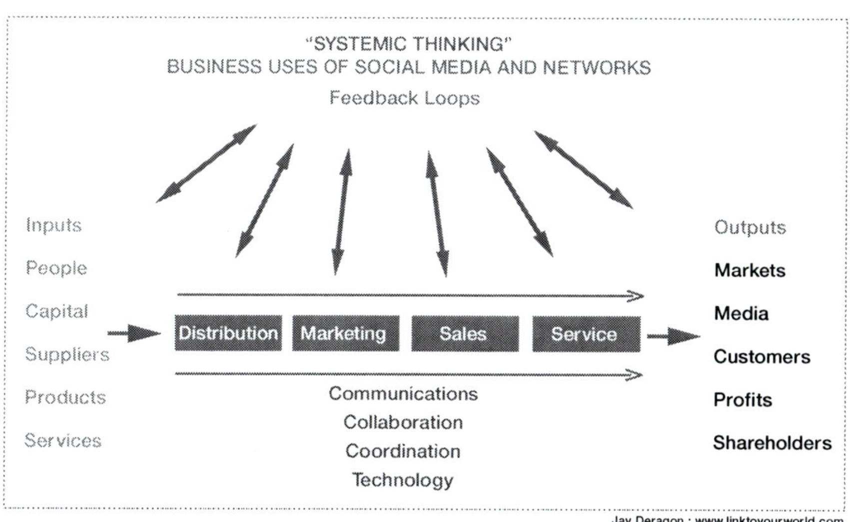

Jay Deragon : www.linktoyourworld.com

The use of social network media and networks is evolving from serving a social need. Now, online social networking services are becoming more popular for business purposes (Jardin, 2007). In addition, users seem to believe that these sites will continue to be useful for business purposes. In response to a poll by MSN, 73 percent of over 4,000 respondents agreed that online social networks can boost business

(2007). An obvious application is to generate sales or business collaboration leads: a salesman can use the service to identify who within his network has the closest links to a prospect, and then request an introduction (2007).

Much of the current emphasis seems to focus on limited application to businesses, and approaches seem to be limited to "silos" of thinking related to recruitment and branding. Businesses may be missing a larger picture of value yet to be tapped and maybe even yet to be envisioned.

"Social networking sounds great in theory, but the business benefits are still unproven," says Paul Jackson of Forrester, a consultancy. "But if who you know really does matter more than what you know, it has obvious potential" (as cited in Jardin, 2007). That has not deterred social networks such as LinkedIn from positioning itself as a professional network. However, some are missing the "systemic" use of social mediums to improve the inputs, processes, and outputs of any business. The diagram represents a macro view of all businesses from the perspective of "Systemic Thinking" or *Systems Thinking* (Senge, 2006).

All business represents a collection of people, processes, and customers. The effectiveness and efficiency of a business is driven by how well the people and processes are connected, managed, and aimed at delivering products and services that satisfy customers. All business requires a medium of marketing, communicating, and selling means that drive customer awareness of the business proposition.

When you view traditional business, systemically one can see how the medium of social networks could and can provide the means for seamless and effective connectivity aimed at delivering the results to the customer efficiently. The medium of social networks provides a new method of reach and richness that can enhance any business. It goes way beyond recruitment of employees and basic Customer Relationship Management applications and cuts across all businesses systemically.

     Chapter 21: The Planning Factors

References

Balanced scorecard. (2007). Retrieved October 29, 2007, from http://en.wikipedia.org/wiki/Balanced_scorecard

Context analysis. (2007, December 21). Retrieved October 29, 2007, from http://en.wikipedia.org/wiki/Context_analysis

Green, H. (2007, September 23). In-House Social Networks: With a nod to Facebook, large companies now have the virtual equivalent of the water cooler on the Web. *BusinessWeek.*
Retrieved October 5, 2007, from www.businessweek.com/managing/content/sep2007/ca20070923_239025.htm http://tinyurl.com/2yvfw2

Jardin, X. (2007). *Online social networks go to work: Where personal connections lead to professional allies.* MSNBC.com. Retrieved October 5, 2007, from http://www.msnbc.msn.com/id/5488683

Morgan, R. A. (2006, March 1). *The Power of Purpose: How can a statistician working in Japan over fifty years ago help your business?* Retrieved October 5, 2007, from http://www.inc.com/resources/office/articles/20060301/morgan.html

Senge, P. M. (2006). *The Fifth Discipline: The Art & Practice of The Learning Organisation* (2nd ed.). Australia: Random House.

Workplace. (2007, October 1). The Water Cooler Is Now On The Web. *BusinessWeek.* Retrieved October 5, 2007, from www.businessweek.com/magazine/content/07_40/b4052072.htm http://tinyurl.com/27jgat

Young, R. (2006, October 9). *The Future of Social Networks—Communication.* Retrieved October 5, 2007, from www.gigaom.com/2006/10/09/the-future-of-social-networks-communication http://tinyurl.com/2e7auk

22 The Future Factors

Jay T. Deragon

Each factor provides an indicator of the future. "The Future Factors" take into consideration the collective meaning of all the factors examined in this book and provide a pathway of strategic thinking that is different from previous strategic thinking methodologies. The medium of social networking both influences and changes most all past paradigms about society, business, politics, and relationships and breathes air into the emergence of The Relationship Economy. We will introduce a new model of strategic thinking using "The Systemic Factors" outlined here and in the future as a model for consideration, when addressing these significant changes.

The progress toward improvements in technology and the ever-increasing demands on time are inevitable. Every day with every new technological evolution in mobile communication, Internet availability, broadband accessibility, etc., the speed of life seems to move incrementally into warp drive. In a paper written in 1968 by Internet pioneers J. C. R. Licklider and Bob Taylor, called "The Computer as a Communication Device," they envisioned the time when real-time interactivity was possible. They expected an acceleration of our abilities to innovate and work creatively. That time is now. Rheingold (2000) envisioned global constellations of change enabled by the Internet.

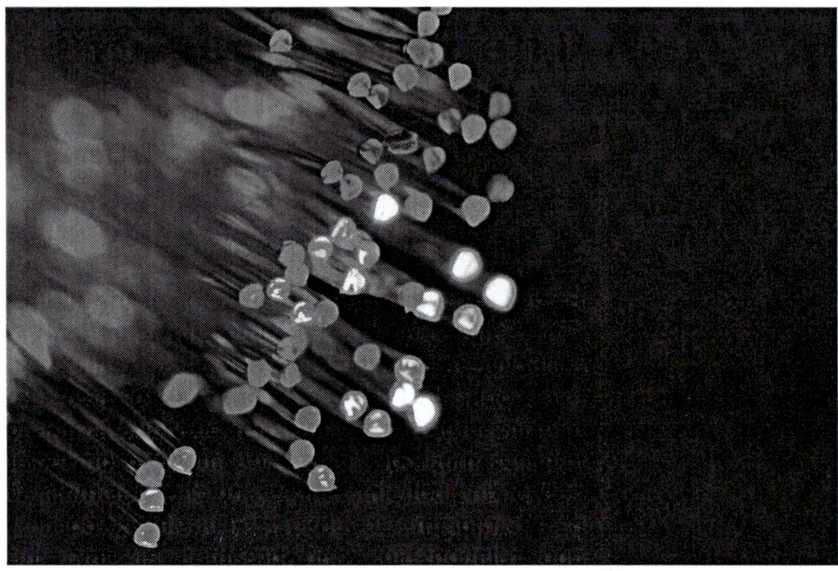

Jan Roger Johannesen, 2007

The Relationship Economy is an economy without borders. The winners of the race will be those who learn faster and are more flexible. Those who succeed in The Relationship Economy will be those who understand it so much that they do not see it as a separate entity (Kelly, 1998). Within The Relationship Economy, the technology is ubiquitous, the economy is migrating to the intangible, and governments are deciding whether legislation is necessary to govern the explosive growth (Kelly, 1998). While the Internet has transformed a variety of local merchants and citizens into a "global village" for information sharing, social interaction, and economic exchange, technology, generally, has allowed for the creation of a new economy (DeFillippi, 2002). What Rheingold (2000) saw in the early 1990s, when the infrastructure for broadband Internet access was still in its infancy, is happening now. He saw entire communities forming, with their inhabitants forming relationships like those in the "real" world (Rheingold, 2000). We are living today what only a few could envision just over a decade ago.

In 2005, 12 young African civic and technology leaders, including the youngest of 1,000 global activist women collectively nominated for the 2005 Nobel Prize, came together in a forum for exploring the social impacts of technology (Sun Press Release, 2005). Sun Microsystems arranged the forum, and Sun's John Gage stated, "People around the world—from New Orleans to Tanzania to Islamabad can use the power of the network to have a huge impact on their society. Together, we will create new direct, person-to-person links to support fundamental change in Africa" (Sun Press Release, 2005). Sun's leadership understood then that the world had dawned on a new era, the "Participation Age," where barriers to technology were diminishing through the proliferation of converged devices, and near-universal connectivity was escalating exponential network engagement (Sun Press Release, 2005).

"From blogs to Java™ technology, SMS messages to Web services, participants are forming communities to drive change, create new business and new social services, and collaborate on new discoveries. This growth in the network economy fueled by interconnected technology will be driven by a commonality of purpose, whether civic, political, or commercial. Sun also believes that sharing and collaboration in the Participation Age will stimulate innovation to help all participants from across the world grow and prosper." (Sun Press Release, 2005)

In 2006, Barnes and Matteson petitioned 453 universities and colleges in the United States to create a comprehensive understanding of uptake of social media. For the approximately 2,000 four-year accredited colleges and universities in the USA, the name of the game is recruiting the best students. Recruiting is a highly competitive process, more like an art than a science, as the controlling factors are usually more subjective than objective and more emotional than logical. In this environment, social media (e.g., blogs, podcasts, message boards, social networking, videos, and wikis) has become an important new marketing tool. Barnes and Mattson (2007) found that generally, the marketing teams of academic institutions are more familiar with and are adopting social media faster (especially blogs) in order to reach technological savvy potential applicants than the Inc 500, which are the 500 fastest growing private companies as designated by Inc. Magazine (Inc.com, 2007). Perhaps more importantly, they are using social media and search engines to research potential students. No longer can applicants behave irresponsibly online without potential consequences to their futures (and their parents' sanity) (Barnes and Mattson, 2007).

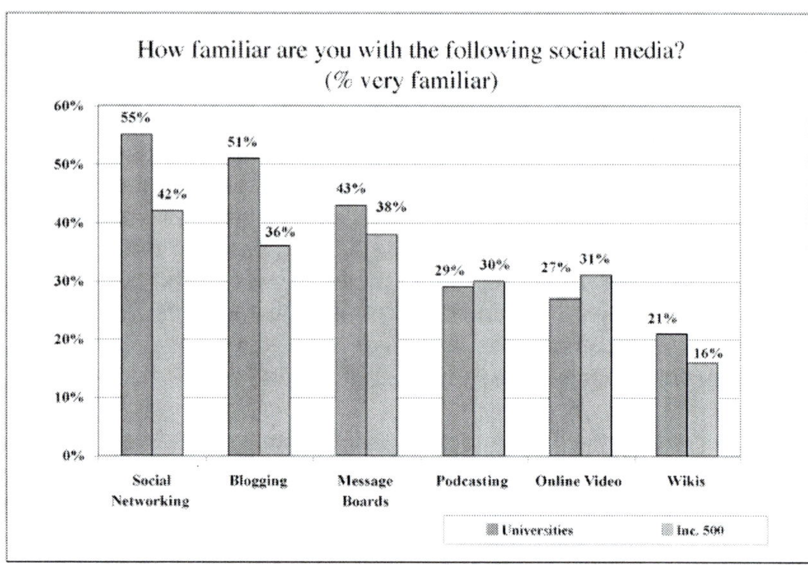

*Figure 8: Social Media Familiarity
(Barnes and Mattson, 2007)*

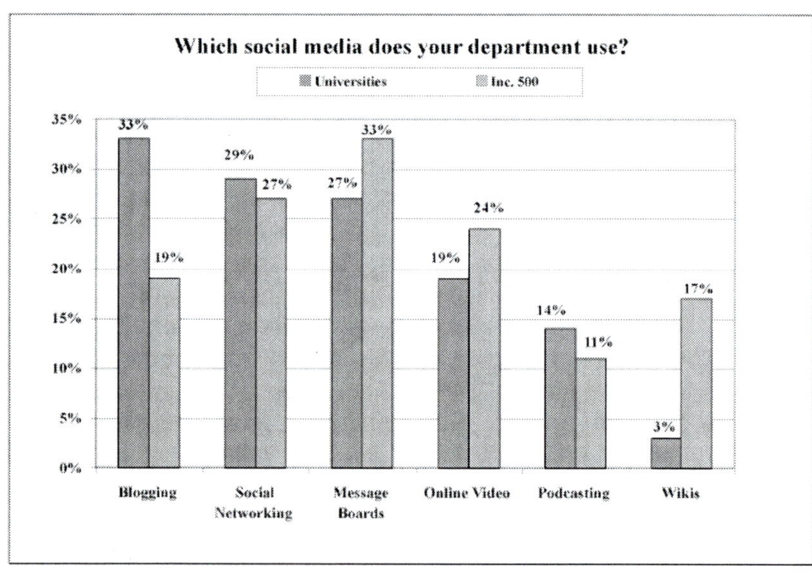

*Figure 9: Social Media by Department
(Barnes and Mattson, 2007)*

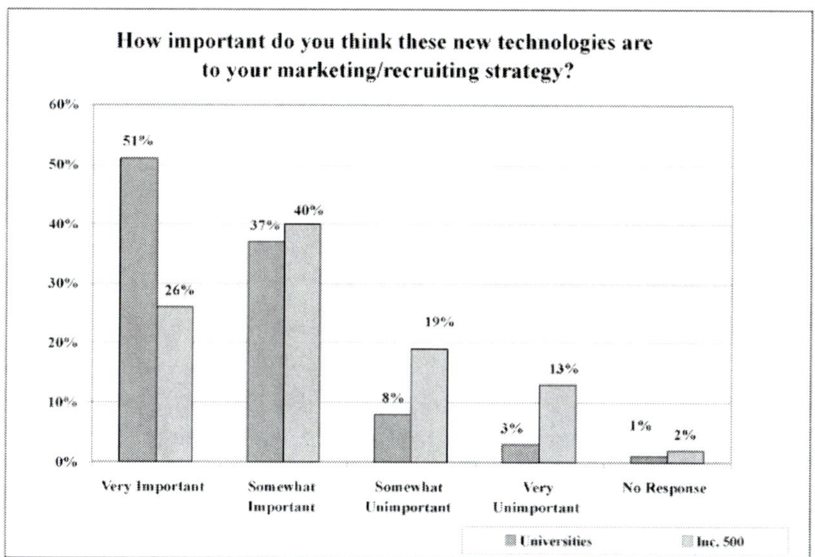

*Figure 10: New Technology for Marketing Strategy
(Barnes and Mattson, 2007)*

For academic recruiting purposes, the social networks represent both the opportunity to have a Web presence though student established alumni groups, as well as for the institution to learn about the students to whom the institution is considering offering admission. Marketing efforts are diffused as traditional approaches such as direct response, television, and radio marketing campaigns now share both potential students' attention and the institutional advertising dollars.

Emerging Organizational Forms

The emerging paradigm of collaborative-networked organizations (CNOs) represents opportunities for a variety of dynamic and multidisciplinary research and development (Camarinha-Matos and Afsarmanesh, 2004). These organizations, similar in structure to social networking communities, will provide valuable elements for research strategy, enabling decision-makers at research funding organizations as well as group leaders in research institutions to fast track and flat cycle new opportunities. Companies interested in innovative development activities in the area of collaborative networking will engage in rapid proto-typing and direct user response capabilities instead of using solutions like focus groups.

In Wikinomics, Don Tapscott and Anthony D. Williams (2006) suggest several directions for the future where self-organization through mass communication will be a norm:

1. Open collaborations to produce collective results not owned by anyone including Wikipedia and Linux.

2. Accessing expert knowledge through idea markets (such as Goldcorp and Proctor & Gamble have done).

3. Customers being able to participate in detailed customization past what the vendor facilitates (effectively creating a blurring of company-customer boundaries).

4. Knowledge transfer among the scientific community.

5. Methods of opening access to partners, especially for complementary software development.

6. Global production methods.

7. New ways of facilitating work in combination with those outside the organization.

Peter Gloor's book, "Swarm Creativity," introduces us to a powerful new concept—Collaborative Innovation Networks, or COINs (Gloor, 2005). His intention was to make the concept of COINs ubiquitous among business managers as any previous methodology used to enhance quality and competitive advantage. Gloor (2005) noted that COINs bear little relationship to previous team models. A COIN is a cyber team of self-motivated people with a collective vision, enabled by technology to collaborate in achieving a common goal—an innovation—by sharing ideas, information, and work (Glorr, 2005). What makes COINs so relevant today is that the networking concept has reached its tipping point—thanks to the Internet and the World Wide Web. Through real-life examples in several business sectors, the Gloor (2005) shows how to leverage COINs to develop successful products in R & D, grow better customer relationships, establish better project management, and build higher-performing teams.

Yet, despite the fact that all these technologies are powerful and widely available, and the fact that using them is becoming almost second nature to all, it remains difficult to deploy useful collaboration tools in the business world—often because of requirement assessment issues, user segmentation issues, training, and usability issues (Kelly, 1998).

In order to implement the available technologies in a way that allows companies to engage in The Relationship Economy, there must be an intentional convergence of technology features, applications, and tools. These convergences must be adaptable and the formulas capable of being changed. If convergence enables more features to be united under a collaboration umbrella, converged tools will become increasingly complex (Delacroix and Gourvennec, 2006). However, the return on investment can be significant. In The Relationship Economy, adaptability is the key, and open collaboration will trump the close-hold proprietary business collaboration models of the past. Breaking the barriers between the various tools that make up collaboration is leading us to this inevitable discussion about convergence (Delacroix and Gourvennec, 2006).

Convergence also describes the unique combination of complementary technologies. According to Henry Jenkins (2006), convergence means the flow of content across multiple media platforms, cooperation between multiple media industries, and the migration of media audiences who are in search of new entertainment experiences and features. Convergence is a word that can be used to describe technological, industrial, cultural, and social changes. In the world of media convergence, every important story is told, every brand is sold, and every consumer is courted across multiple media platforms. Currently, the culture of convergence is defined from two dynamically different perspectives—top-down from the corporate boardrooms and bottom-up by the most active users, which are teenagers. Convergence is shaped by the desires to expand media empires across multiple platforms and by the desires of consumers to have the media they want—where they want it, when they want it, and in the format they want (Jenkins, 2006).

In a culture that provides what some have described as information overload, it is impossible for any one of us to hold all of the relevant pieces of information in our heads at the same time (Jenkins, 2006).

Because there is more information available on any given topic than we can store in our heads, there is an additional incentive for us to talk about the media we consume, and this conversation creates buzz and accelerates the circulation of media content (Jenkins, 2006). Information consumption has become a collective process and has defined the term *collective intelligence*. None of us can know everything; each of us knows something; we can put the pieces together if we pool our resources and combine our skills (Jenkins, 2006). Collective intelligence can be seen as an alternative source of media power, and we are learning how to use that power through our day-to-day interactions within convergence culture. We are using collective power through our recreational life, but it has implications at all levels of our culture. There is a cultural shift that is occurring as consumers fight for control across disparate channels, changing the way we do business, elect our leaders, and educate our children (Jenkins, 2006).

To quote Victor Hugo, "You can resist an invading army, but you cannot resist an idea whose time has come."

Enter Web 2.0 and the Social Web

Table 9:   Monthly Unique Visitors (comScore, 2007)

Worldwide Growth of Selected Social Networking Sites June 2007 vs. June 2006 Total Worldwide Home/Work Locations Among Internet Users Age 15+ Source: comScore World Metrix			
	Total Unique Visitors (000)		
Social Networking Site	**Jun-06**	**Jun-07**	**% Change**
MySpace	66,401	114,147	72
Facebook	14,083	52,167	270
Hi5	18,098	28,174	56
Friendster	14,917	24,675	65
Orkut	13,588	24,120	78
Bebo	6,694	18,200	172
Tagged	1,506	13,167	774

Table 10:   Average Daily Unique Visitors (comScore, 2007)

Worldwide Daily Visitation of Selected Social Networking Sites June 2007 vs. June 2006 Total Worldwide Home/Work Locations Among Internet Users Age 15+ Source: comScore World Metrix			
Social Networking Site	**Average Daily Visitors (000)**		
	Jun-06	**Jun-07**	**% Change**
MySpace	16,764	28,786	72
Facebook	3,742	14,917	299
Hi5	2,873	4,727	65
Friendster	3,037	5,966	96
Orkut	5,488	9,628	75
Bebo	1,188	4,833	307
Tagged	202	983	386

- Top 20 social networking websites accounted for 3.6 percent of upstream visits to Shopping & Classified Sites in May 2007, increased 86.7 percent since May 2006.

- MySpace, the leading social network, accounted for 3.2 percent of upstream visits to Shopping $Classifieds websites in May 2007.

In the previous generation of the Web, portals dominated the traffic by providing consumers access to things. Advertisers followed dominant traffic sites like Yahoo, MSN, Google, etc. Those portals gave people unlimited and instantaneous access to media and information. The search capabilities incorporated into the portals enabled people to find what they were looking for with ease and speed.

That Web provided data rich information about what people searched for and where people were "surfing and landing" from most to least. The data enabled the media and marketers to target people with a reach that extended far beyond traditional methods. Advertisers flocked to the Web with the promise of improved "clickthroughs" by using advanced technologies aimed at the preferences of various target audiences.

When Web 2.0 was introduced, it brought a new dynamic to the marketplace—people connecting with people. People finding and connecting with people has become more important than finding and connecting to "things." The social Web has emerged quickly and the traffic patterns created by it have created new dynamics for media.

Users of the social Web are finding new meaning in the use and application of technology as a means to establish extended relationships for numerous purposes. Self-expression and affinity to content, causes, ideas and propositions presented by people from around the globe has become a major attraction to "The Human Network."

Social networks are the fastest growing segment on the Web. Geographic, industry, topical and a proliferation of other categories of interest are showing up in the form of social networks at explosive rates. In this new economy, the BIG (corporations, media, big business, etc.) compete with the SMALL (small businesses, organizations, and individuals). The new medium provides a significant advantage to the small. Facebook's success has attracted the BIG, and the debate as to which strategies will enable what companies to be tomorrow's leaders of the social Web have become the mainstream topics of the media.

Michael Pokocky, Copyright © 2007

Of course, there are also those that discount the shifts created by the social Web as hype or temporary fads fueled by the youth's attraction to MySpace. Whatever their opinion, they cannot ignore the data and its potential meaning, nor can they ignore the accelerated rate of technological advancements.

Conclusion

It is relatively easy for individuals to identify what they believe is lacking in social network systems, technology, and applications. However, the rapid technological evolution makes it is apparent that any wish is, most likely, already in the development stage. Because the medium of social networking accelerates human interaction across all divides, the demands on it cause it to evolve faster each successive year. For example, the evolution of ideas and applications are evident from the rapid growth of Facebook, to the proliferation of applications available to its users, to the availability of source code.

These interactions are creating exchanges of thoughts, ideas, and emotions. One can expect that this acceleration of exchanges will introduce new dynamics of creativity and connectivity and possibilities never before anticipated, experienced, or expected. There is a pathway to abundance with no boundaries—one that is beyond today's comprehension or definition of any other form of communication and transmission of ideas and content in the history of our existence. A new era has been born—that of the human network—and it enables individuals to share thoughts, emotions, and ideas to a wider audience than ever before.

The Human Network cannot be ignored. People connecting with people has been and will always be a dynamic force that has the power to change markets, world events, history, business, religion, politics, and economics to name just a few. The explosive growth of The Relationship Economy is due to the continuing expansion of The Human Network. To stay abreast of the curve requires continuing exposure and experience in social networks and a realization that this industry—the social media industry—is life altering and will continue to impact business, government, and organizations.

References

Barnes, N. and Mattson, E. (2007). U. Mass. Dartmouth Center for Marketing Research. *The Game Has Changed: College Admissions Outpace Corporations in Embracing Social Media.* Dr. Nora Ganim Barnes and Eric Mattson.

Camarinha-Matos, L. M. and Afsarmanesh, H. (2004). *Collaborative Networked Organizations: A research agenda for emerging business models.* Berkeley, CA: Springer.

comScore, Inc. (2007, July 31). Tables 9 and 10 Used with Permission. Retrieved December 25, 2007 from http://www.comscore.com/press/release.asp?press=1555

DeFillippi, R. J. (2002). Information technology and organizational models for project collaboration in the new economy. *Human Resource Planning,* 25(4).

Delacroix, J. and Gourvennec, Y. (2006). *Relationship Intelligence Management: A new paradigm.* Retrieved October 10, 2007, from www.cooperatics.wordpress.com/2006/01/09/ relationship-intelligence-management-a-new-paradigm http://tinyurl.com/2hhonw

Gloor, P. A. (2005). *Swarm Creativity: Competitive advantage through collaborative innovation networks.* New York: Oxford University Press.

Jenkins, J. (2006). *Convergence culture: Where old and new media collide.* New York: New York University Press.

Kelly, K. (1998). *New Rules for the New Economy.* Retrieved September 1, 2007, from http://www.kk.org/newrules

Pokocky, Michael (2007). Sketches used by permission. All rights reserved and provided with gracious permission to use by the authors of this book.

Rheingold, H. (2000). *The virtual community: Homesteading on the electronic frontier.* Cambridge, MA: The MIT Press.

Sun Press Release (2005, October 11). *Sun participation fellows to engage in roundtable discussion on use of technology for social and economic advancement in Africa.* Retrieved October 10, 2007, from www.sun.com/smi/Press/sunflash/2005-10/sunflash.20051011.1.xml http://tinyurl.com/2g6wde

Tapscott, D. and Williams, A. D. (2006). Wikinomics: *How mass collaboration changes everything.* New York: Portfolio.

Conclusion

Conventional business thinking has historically focused on producing, distributing, marketing, selling, and serving customers with unique value propositions and messages.

Conventional business models have been centered on structured organizational designs aimed at optimizing productivity, controlling cost and improving quality.

Conventional business wisdom has focused on selling more at less cost while expanding markets and staying true to core competencies.

Today's business environment faces many challenges. The challenges include finding, training, and keeping talented employees; managing increasing cost of technological advances; adjusting to global competition, shifting market dynamics, the fluctuating cost of money; and the list continues.

The impact of social networks on businesses will call for new thinking necessary to succeed in a connected and challenging world. Today, conventional wisdom cannot help you keep pace with the rapidly changing business landscape, and outmoded structures, models, and methods can actually lead you to obsolescence and failure. Today, business people have to turn the old rules inside out, upside down, and backwards not only to succeed, but also to survive!

The rules of business are changing. The new rules are unconventional.

The social Web removes all barriers to entry, provides technological mediums at a fraction of historical costs, enables people to work from anywhere at any time, and connects everyone to everything global-ly—including customers—at the click of the mouse.

Companies and their leaders that fail to capitalize on the opportunities of the social Web will lose market share that may ultimately reduce shareholder value. The real sources of future business success will be centered on the knowledge and creativity of how to tap into and use the power of the social Web for business purposes. The social Web chal-lenges conventional wisdom, while providing data, resources, and insights to help companies transition to the unconventional wisdom of networks as capital and human resources.

The social Web is the future business landscape that could enable businesses to produce much higher returns than conventional business structures and models. Understanding the dynamics of the social Web forces businesses to challenge questionable assumptions and much conventional management wisdom.

The social Web enables businesses to access a global reach of rich ideas and resources. Networks will fuel dramatic changes in business structures and dramatic changes in the idea of collaboration and sharing with unimaginable communities as sources of ideas. Given this access, all kinds of people can get involved in business challenges and "discover gold" from unimaginable sources—via sharing a bit of infor-mation.

Looking from the Outside in

While conversations about businesses adopting the social Web seem to be accelerating, most of the observations and context of these dis-cussions have been through the lens of looking from the inside out. The failure of businesses to view the dynamics of the social Web from the outside in is the transformational constraint of many and the explosive opportunity for the few.

Looking at the social Web from within the existing context of business limits the ability to gain an objective view of the future. In this dynamic social media space, there is always movement coming over the horizon, yet sometimes all we can see is a cloud of dust being kicked up once again by old thinking.

Thinking tends to be molded over time by environmental influences such as business rules and the mental models learned from experience. This vantage point—from the inside out—is often limited by the paradigms of experience, the lack of outside knowledge, and limited vantage points. For businesses to maximize the opportunity of the medium of social networks, they will need to gain a perspective from the outside in.

As the media reports more and more about innovative uses of social networks for business purposes, the old mental models will be pushed from the outside in. The analyst, consultants, and market makers will create the new paradigms which will be adopted by businesses globally.

The failure of businesses to view the dynamics of the social Web from the outside in is the transformational constraint of many—and the explosive opportunity for the few.

Doc Searls states:

> "Most corporations only know how to talk in the soothing, humorless monotone of the mission statement, marketing brochure, and your-call-is-important-to-us busy signal. Same old tone, same old lies. No wonder networked markets have no respect for companies unable or unwilling to speak as they do. But learning to speak in a human voice is not some trick, nor will corporations convince us they are human with lip service about "listening to customers." They will only sound human when they empower real human beings to speak on their behalf."

> "While many such people already work for companies today, most companies ignore their ability to deliver genuine knowledge, opting instead to crank out sterile happy talk that insults the intelligence of markets literally too smart to buy it."

"However, employees are getting hyperlinked even as markets are. Companies need to listen carefully to both. Mostly, they need to get out of the way so intranetworked employees can converse directly with internetworked markets."

"Corporate firewalls have kept smart employees in and smart markets out. It's going to cause real pain to tear those walls down. But the result will be a new kind of conversation. And it will be the most exciting conversation business has ever engaged in." (2007)

Leapfrogging will Accelerate Adoption

Leapfrogging (the strategy of jumping over and ahead of your competition) will be the tipping point that will accelerate the entry of entire industries globally into the social Web. As soon as a company, large or small, leverages the social Web for strategic advantage and the media writes about its success, entire industries will shift like a California wildfire coming over the hill.

Leapfrogging requires leaders to look way ahead of current trends and capabilities and create strategies unforeseen and unknowable to current market dynamics. Leapfrogging requires faith and confidence in technological advances with the ability to envision possibilities yet realized. Leaders are those gifted with a keen eye on the future and the ability to pave a road that brings their entire organization, if not their entire industry, to new futures that will be enabled by the social Web.

This book has provided the foundational knowledge of the initial factors that are the critical influences of thinking about the social Web. What you do with the foundation is of strategic importance—you can crawl or leap. Choose wisely.

Reference

Searls, D. (2007). Building an Relationship Economy. http://www.linuxjournal.com/node/1000182 referencing *The Cluetrain Manifesto,* Retrieved October 17, 2007, from http://cluetrain.com

About the Authors

Scott Allen

Scott Allen is Co-Founder and Managing Partner of Link to Your World, LLC
http://www.linktoyourworld.com
a full-service company that helps organizations transform virtual relationships into real business. He is co-author of *The Virtual Handshake: Opening Doors and Closing Deals Online* and a contributing author and editor of numerous books on the topic of social networking and social media.

Mr. Allen is the Entrepreneurs Guide for *About.com*, a subsidiary of The New York Times Company and one of the top ten content websites in the world. He is a monthly columnist and expert blogger for FastCompany.com and a contributing expert at Work.com, In addition, he blogs at

- TheVirtualHandshake.com
  http://www.thevirtualhandshake.com and

- LinkedIntelligence.com
  http://linkedintelligence.com

Jay T. Deragon

Jay Deragon is Co-Founder and Managing Partner of Link to Your World, LLC
http://www.linktoyourworld.com
as well as co-founder of various networks including:

- Link to New York
  http://www.linktonewyork.com and

- Link to Wall Street
  http://www.linktowallstreet.com

In addition, he founded Wireless Factors, http://www.wirelessfactors.com, that serves the networking needs of the global Wireless Communications Community.

Mr. Deragon is considered one of the premier entrepreneurial thought leaders in the dynamic social networking space and the emerging industry of social networks. His blog—
http://www.relationship-economy.com
serves as a reference point for the emerging industry of social networks. He has had a successful career as a serial entrepreneur—founding, operating, and selling numerous businesses.

Margaret G. Orem

Margaret Orem is Co-Founder and Managing Partner of Link to Your World, LLC http://www.linktoyourworld.com and Founder and CEO of Execsolution, Inc. http://www.execsolution.com. In addition to serving as a Board Member of the International Debate Education Association-US–http://www.idebate.org, she is a co-founder of various social networks including

- Link to New York http://www.linktonewyork.com and

- Link to Wall Street http://www.linktowallstreet.com

Ms. Orem is an entrepreneur with CEO operational experience in going concerns, start-up businesses, and troubled companies. With a foundation in government, public, private, and non-profit entities, she has expertise in both restructuring and building new and existing enterprises.

Carter F. Smith

Carter Smith is Senior Partner of Link to Your World, LLC
http://www.linktoyourworld.com
In addition, he is an Adjunct Professor at Austin Peay State University, and Mountain State University, and a S.T.A.R. Instructor for the Federal Law Enforcement Training Center, part of the U. S. Department of Homeland Security. He has adopted the edutainment teaching style, using a variety of platforms, including social media, to enhance learning and facilitate comprehension.

Mr. Smith is an educator, trainer, strategic networker, and facilitator with a background in government, and non-profit and for-profit organizations. He has presented and taught a variety of topics in individual and cohort settings, face-to-face and online environments, and national and international media forums. In addition, he is a founding board member of the Tennessee Gang Investigators Association http://www.tn-gia.org and Square One Ranch http://www.squareoneranch.org.

A Message from Happy About®

Thank you for your purchase of *The Emergence of The Relationship Economy*—it is available online at http://happyabout.info/RelationshipEconomy.php or at other online and physical bookstores.

- Please contact us for quantity discounts at sales@happyabout.info
- If you want to be informed by e-mail of upcoming Happy About® books, please e-mail bookupdate@happyabout.info.

Happy About is interested in you if you are an author who would like to submit a non-fiction book proposal or a corporation that would like to have a book written for you. Please contact us by e-mail at editorial@happyabout.info or phone (1-408-257-3000).

Other books relating to the Relationship Economy:

- Collaboration 2.0:
  http://happyabout.info/collaboration2.0.php
- I'm on Facebook — Now What???
  http://happyabout.info/facebook.php
- I'm on LinkedIn — Now What???
  http://happyabout.info/linkedinhelp.php
- Happy About Online Networking:
  http://happyabout.info/onlinenetworking.php
- Tales From the Networking Community:
  http://www.happyabout.info/networking-community.php
- Internet Your Way to a New Job:
  http://www.happyabout.info/InternetYourWaytoaNewJob.php
- Marketing Thought:
  http://www.happyabout.info/MarketingThought.php
- Rule #1: Stop Talking! A Guide to Listening:
  http://happyabout.info/listenerspress/stoptalking.php
- 42 Rules of Marketing:
  http://happyabout.info/42rules/marketing.php
- Overcoming Inventoritis:
  http://happyabout.info/overcoming-inventoritis.php

To purchase *The Emergence of The Relationship Economy* or other Happy About books, order online or by phone 1-408-257-3000, go to your local book store, or fill out this order form and send it with payment to:

Happy About
20660 Stevens Creek Blvd.
Suite 210
Cupertino, CA 95014

Available online:
http://happyabout.info/books.php

— —

Name____

Address____

City _________________ State ______________ Zip___________

Qty

❑ The Emergence of The Relationship Economy ($21.95/ea) __ _______
❑ Collaboration 2.0 ($29.95/ea) __ _______
❑ I'm on Facebook — Now What??? ($19.95/ea) __ _______
❑ I'm on LinkedIn — Now What??? ($19.95/ea) __ _______
❑ Happy About Online Networking ($19.95/ea) __ _______
❑ Tales From the Networking Community ($19.95/ea) __ _______
❑ Internet Your Way to a New Job ($19.95/ea) __ _______
❑ Marketing Thought ($19.95/ea) __ _______
❑ Rule #1: Stop Talking! A Guide to Listening ($16.95/ea) __ _______
❑ 42 Rules of Marketing ($19.95/ea) __ _______
❑ Overcoming Inventoritis ($19.95/ea) __ _______

Book Total _______________

Tax (CA +8.25%) _______________

Shipping ($5.95 1st book, .75 ea add'l book) _______________

Total _______________

❑ Check enclosed   ❑ Credit Card (type) _______________________

Credit Card # ______________________ Exp. date___________

Name on card ______________Signature _____________________